Tell Me Your Story

The Parables of Jesus

Tell Me Your Story

The Parables of Jesus

Arthur E. Zannoni

LITURGY
TRAINING
PUBLICATIONS

TELL ME YOUR STORY: THE PARABLES OF JESUS © 2002 Archdiocese of Chicago: Liturgy Training Publications, 1800 North Hermitage Avenue, Chicago IL 60622-1101; 1-800-933-1800, fax 1-800-933-7094, e-mail orders@ltp.org. All rights reserved. Visit our website at www.ltp.org.

This book was edited by Victoria M. Tufano. Kris Fankhouser was the production editor. The design is by Larry Cope, and the typesetting was done by Jim Mellody-Pizzato in Palatino and Papyrus. Printed by Webcom in Toronto, Canada. The illustrations are by Julie Lonneman. The index was compiled by Elizabeth Anders.

Library of Congress Control Number: 2001097504

ISBN 1-56854-413-8

STORY

THIS BOOK IS DEDICATED TO OUR MOTHERS

Grace Evelyn Gilkerson Flannery

(1918–2000)

Stella Marie Scarano Zannoni

(1918–1999)

Table of Contents

ACKNOWLEDGMENTS

We have all heard that it takes an entire village to raise a child. The same is true in writing a book. No book is ever the result of only the author's hard work, but rather a project that involves many loving and caring people.

For encouragement when things became tough, I want to thank my son Luke, my daughter Laura and fellow writers and friends David Haas, Bill Huebsch and Kevin Perrotta. Special thanks go to Marcia Berra and Maureen Seavey, who graciously volunteered to read the entire manuscript and who offered invaluable suggestions and diligently checked all of the Bible references. Their hard work helped improve the overall quality of the book.

I want to thank all of the editors and design people at Liturgy Training Publications, especially Victoria Tufano for her friendship and the countless hours of carefully editing the original manuscript. All of her changes, additions and deletions have improved the quality of the book. Appreciation is also expressed to Leslie Carney for her professional expertise and diligence in typing the entire manuscript after numerous edits.

Finally, in a profoundly heartfelt way, I want to thank my spouse and beloved, Kathleen Flannery Zannoni, who affirmed my need to write and who supported me with encouragement, prayer and extra hours of loving care of our three-year-old son Alessandro, allowing me time to write. She is like the capable spouse described in the book of Proverbs: "Many women have done excellently, but you surpass them all" (Proverbs 31:29).

Introduction

I have yet to meet a person who does not like a good story. As a child, I loved hearing the stories of my parents and grandparents—not the ones they read to me out of books, but the ones they told from memory or made up as they told them. These stories captured my imagination. From my youngest days, the phrase "Once upon a time" is engraved on my consciousness.

When I was in elementary school, my teachers would both tell me and read me stories. As a child, I loved going to the library and listening to the stories the librarian read to us children. These stories inspired my spirit of wonder and adventure. I soon learned that stories were the envelopes that carried fantastic messages and deep wisdom.

When I was in college, my professors often laced their lectures with stories. I also began to notice that public speakers frequently began with an anecdote or story to relax the audience and to whet their appetites for the message they were about to present. Further, I observed that politicians tried to sway undecided voters by means of a story or two, and parents always provided their children with stories to help them remember other family members and events.

Children always expect a bedtime story. As the father of three children, I have told and read countless stories and watched my own children's eyes light up with excitement, wonder and awe as they listened intently, often cuddled up under the bedcovers with me.

In many cultures, even today, the storyteller is a highly respected person. The storyteller is the keeper of the community's myths, which are, of course, any culture's deepest expressions of meaning. Second perhaps only to the priest or shaman, the storyteller in any society paints on the canvas of imagination with words whose colors are as vivid as those used by any visual artist and whose meaning lives on.

One of history's most capable storytellers was a young, itinerant Galilean rabbi named Jesus of Nazareth, whose stories are known as parables. While none of his disciples ever asked him to tell a story, Jesus nonetheless told many. In every generation since his death and resurrection, his followers have told and shared these stories. The story of Jesus and the stories he told are in many ways the very heart of Christian belief.

The parables of Jesus continue to intrigue, inspire, puzzle, challenge and amuse all who encounter them. They are the basis for sermons in Christian churches around the world, and they are the first stories of Jesus that are taught to children.

Parables have inspired poets, painters, and playwrights, who have often used them as the basis for their own work.

While the gospels report both stories about Jesus, and the stories that Jesus told, this book is limited to looking at some of the stories that Jesus told. Specifically, the book will look at some of the parables found in the synoptic gospels. John's gospel will not be discussed because it does not contain parables.

Chapter 1 sets the stage for the entire book as it explores the relationship between the stories of Jesus and our own stories. It shows that the meaning of parables not only transcends time and space, but relates in an important way to the practice of discipleship.

In chapter 2, the reader is introduced to the parables of Jesus, their origin and background, their content and context. In addition, suggestions are offered on how to read a parable, paying close attention to characters and style.

Chapter 3 begins with a short background on the gospel of Mark and then looks at the parables of the kingdom in that gospel. In the first part of this chapter, a suggestion is offered for wrestling with the meaning of the phrase "the kingdom of God." The second part deals with the kingdom parables found in Mark.

Both background and selected parables from the gospel of Matthew form the topic of chapter 4. This chapter does not look at every parable in Matthew's gospel, but rather addresses the kingdom parables first, then looks at a selection of other parables from the gospel.

After a detailed introduction to the gospel of Luke, chapter 5 centers around the parables of the kingdom found in the Third Gospel. Chapters 6 through 10 deal with themes that are found in the parables. The theme of God, his love and forgiveness are explored in chapter 6, while chapter 7 reflects on parables that deal with poverty and riches. Since prayer is such an integral part of Christian life, chapter 8 reflects on three parables about prayer. Jesus' parables about forgiveness, table fellowship and compassion are discussed in chapter 9. Following Jesus, or the call to be a disciple as narrated in the parables, is the theme of chapter 10.

After the analysis of a parable or group of parables, "points for reflection" are offered to help the reader apply the meaning and challenges of the parable(s) being interpreted to his or her own life and practice of faith. In addition, discussion questions are found at the end of each chapter. You may want to look at these before reading a particular chapter, for they can help you better grasp key points. For those who want to do more study or reading on the parables, a select bibliography is provided at the end of the book.

Since the parables of Jesus, for most Catholic Christians, are encountered at the celebration of the eucharist, a list based on the three-year cycle of readings from the lectionary is provided. It specifies when a particular parable has been chosen to be read at Mass, either on Sunday or during the week.

This book hopes to involve the reader with God, Jesus and his life as revealed through the parables. Because it is written for the non-specialist, no attempt is made to be encyclopedic about the gospel parables. The modest goals of this book are to acquaint the reader with the parables and to inspire reflection on and prayer with these stories that Jesus left behind.

I hope this book helps everyone take seriously the role of the Bible in developing one's faith. At the dawn of the twenty-first century, the light of the parables can still dispel the darkness of fear and ignorance. Ignorance must never be celebrated—it must always be challenged. As St. Jerome so aptly stated, "Ignorance of the Scriptures is ignorance of Christ."

Finally, I would challenge all who read this book to approach the parables of Jesus recorded in the synoptic gospels as instances of a "performative utterance," that is, as words that intend to effect the reality of which they speak. For the parables still carry with them a challenge to hear the voice of Jesus in the words of the evangelists, and to hear in Jesus' words the voice of God. How individual readers hear these words and whose voice they hear within them is precisely the challenge of Jesus' stories.

Soli Deo Gloria

Jesus' Story and Our Stories

"The story of Jesus carries the struggles
and hopes of all our stories."

(John Shea)[1]

While I was writing this book, a friend quipped, "Another book on parables, who needs it? After all, aren't Jesus' parables pleasant-sounding fables about human situations long past? What present-day meaning could they possibly have?" This disconcerting remark forced me to reflect long and hard on the relevance of the parables for today. I recalled the adage that "assumptions are the Achilles' heel of every argument." So allow me to reveal the assumptions upon which this book rests.

Chapter One

This book begins with the premise that the Bible is the inspired revelation of God and that the reader finds the Bible meaningful and makes use of it as a guide for his or her daily life. It understands that the Bible is normative for faith, always taking the Bible seriously but not necessarily literally. This book presumes that if the reader is a Christian, then that person is seeking to emulate Jesus—his person, life and teachings.

This book further assumes that stories are a key means for learning about and living life. The story of Jesus and the stories that he told (the parables) are media for the message of the divine. They are not simply the envelopes that carry the message—they are the message itself. Parables are symbolic expressions of meaning about the experience of God, Jesus and our fellow human beings. They cause us to pause, ponder and act on what they mean. A person of faith who encounters the parables of Jesus does not remain unchanged. At certain times, the story of Jesus and the individual's story intersect. Reflecting on this intersection helps a person both to struggle with and to practice faith.

This was made clear to me recently while participating in a retreat. We were seated in a circle and the retreat director faced each of us individually and asked, "Tell me your story." As we listened it became evident that each of us had different yet similar stories, and often our own stories related to Jesus' stories, the parables. Some of us considered ourselves the prodigal son or daughter who had received God's compassionate forgiveness (Luke 15:11–32). Others felt they were the lost sheep that God searched for and found (Luke 15:3–7). Still others pondered how mysteriously God's grace worked in them, like the yeast that the woman mixed into her dough (Luke 13:20–21; Matthew 13:33). One man spent over a quarter of his life searching for God; he felt like the merchant who found the precious pearl (Matthew 13:45–46). Another woman shared that the treasure she found while digging up her past was the importance of God in her life, and for that she would be willing to sell everything she had (Matthew 13:44). A college student, while on a winter school vacation, was stranded in her car in a snowdrift in subzero weather, and was rescued by an elderly couple who, for her, were living examples of the compassionate Samaritan (Luke 10:25–37).

Jesus' whole life was a story. So is ours. He left stories behind for others to ponder and enjoy. So do we. He was remembered for his stories. So are we. Our stories continue to be told, often within the context of a meal, and preserved by our families. The stories of Jesus were and continue to be told and preserved by the community of faith, the church. Moreover, the church proclaims and dines with these stories in the celebration of the eucharist. The church tells the story of Jesus over and over again because it is so good, just as we tell our family stories over and over again. They do not get stale or corny, as jokes do. Like good wine, Jesus' parables get better with time.

Wine is a living substance; it causes the mind and heart to grow fond. The Romans used to say *in vino veritas,* in wine there is truth. The parables are the living word of God, where truth can be discovered. Like Pontius Pilate in the gospels, we all ask the question, "What is truth?" (John 18:37). Unlike Pilate, we recognize that

Jesus is the one who "came into the world, to testify to the truth" (John 18:37). Jesus' witness to the truth was the life he lived, including the parables he told.

It is easy to keep the meaning of the parables at arm's length by limiting their relevance to the historical and cultural time of Jesus. But people who read the gospels seriously know that when reading a parable one always asks, "What is its meaning—for then, for now, for always?"

Parables for Then

All of the parables are historically and culturally conditioned. When Jesus originally told them, they had meaning for his immediate audience. Each of the gospel writers had a particular meaning in mind for his readers when he wrote it down. This would be the meaning behind the text of the parable. Sometimes Jesus shocked his original audience by comparing God to a woman who searches for a lost coin (Luke 15:8–10) or to a woman who mixes yeast into dough (Matthew 13:33; Luke 13:20–21) or by presenting God as a compassionate Samaritan (Luke 10:25–37). Less shocking would have been the parables Jesus told of the sower and the seed (Mark 4:1–29), the great banquet (Matthew 22:1–14) and the bridesmaids (Matthew 25:1–13). These were all images and metaphors that Jesus' original audience would have immediately understood.

Parables for Now

Limiting the meaning of Jesus' parables to their original time and culture, however, would be a great disservice. It would also reduce the parables to antiquated period pieces. The parables of Jesus continue to have meaning today.

Jesus is most fully and consistently encountered within the context of the believing community of the church, because the risen Lord identifies himself with this community. Jesus is "life-giving Spirit" (1 Corinthians 15:45) most directly for those who have entered, by their baptism and by their "drinking of the Spirit" (1 Corinthians 12:13), into the life that is Jesus' continuing presence in the world. Jesus promised in Matthew 18:20, "For where two or three are gathered in my name, I am there among them," and told the disciples, "And remember, I am with you always to the end of the age" (Matthew 28:20). One of the places where Jesus remains with us is in the stories he left for us—the parables.

People of faith today, like those of the past, want to know how persistent they should be in prayer. Reading and hearing the parable of the persistent widow (Luke 18:1–8) will help them maintain their persistence. Others want to know if God hears prayers. Encountering the parable of the friend at midnight (Luke 11:5–13) will give them a response. Contemporary people of faith want to know what they need to do to enjoy ultimate union with God. The parable of the last judgment (Matthew 25:31–46) gives them a good idea. Another contemporary concern is knowing that one is forgiven by God for the mistakes one makes. The parables of

God's extraordinary forgiveness (Matthew 18:23–35) and the forgiveness by the father of the prodigal son (Luke 15:11–32) address this concern.

Parables have meaning for today not because they need to be made relevant by us (that was done by Jesus), but because they continue to address the issues and situations that we all encounter on the pilgrimage of life. Parables do not provide information for living as much as they provide inspiration for living. They inspire us to ponder anew who we are and what is required of us by God.

Parables for Always

Parables are open-ended stories. It is up to the hearer or reader to complete their meaning: "Let anyone with ears to hear listen!" (Mark 4:9). The meaning of Jesus' parables transcends time and culture, gender and ethnic identity. There is a universal appeal to Jesus' parables, if only in the sense that they raise deep and important questions: Where is our treasure? What kind of ground do we provide for the seed of God? What price are we willing to pay for the reign of God in our hearts and minds? What does it mean to forgive? What does it mean to be compassionate? How does one become a gracious receiver of God's grace?

There is a certain eternal quality to the gospel parables because they are all concerned about God, justice and mercy, which are never limited to one age or era. Parables require every human generation to look at how poverty and wealth impinge on the practice of justice and faith. Furthermore, parables do not simply recount a clever tale; rather they prick away at a person's conscience, causing reflection and at times discomfort, but always calling one to action.

The stories of Jesus have the fingerprints of all who have handled them in the past, and they provide hope and inspiration for those who will receive them in the future. We always stand on the faith of those who have gone before us: our parents who first offered us Jesus' stories as well as the saints of the church whose lives are based on the Jesus story. But we also provide hope for those who will live after us by sharing the parables of Jesus with them.

The Parables and Discipleship

The parables challenge the listener in every age to become a disciple of Jesus. Commenting on this, Dietrich Bonhoeffer said, "There is no road to faith or discipleship, no other road—only obedience to the call of Jesus."[2] After hearing the call, one must follow. Discipleship as described in the gospels is a following after Jesus, a journeying with him. The purpose of discipleship is to learn how to live life from the Master whose lifestyle reveals God's goodness, care and compassion toward all human beings.

Journeying with Jesus means traveling on the road of life with him and following his way of life. "Jesus demands an immense trust in him."[3] Such trust requires a disciple to become an itinerant, a sojourner; to have nowhere to lay one's head, no permanent resting place. It means undertaking the journey from the life of conventional wisdom to the life of the real wisdom of the Spirit. To journey with Jesus means listening to his teachings conveyed in the parables—sometimes understanding these teachings, sometimes not quite getting it. This journey can also involve denying or doubting Jesus or even betraying him. Regardless, the journey is in his company, in his presence.

Along the way we are fed and nourished by Jesus' parables, breaking them open just as we break bread and feasting on their meaning. This is the banquet Jesus provides for all of his followers. It is an inclusive banquet, including not just me and not just us, but those we tend to exclude, those who in the parables are referred to as the lost sheep whom God seeks.

Discipleship is a community affair. To be a disciple is to become part of the alternative community of Jesus, the church. It is the road less traveled, but never traveled alone. Discipleship is not a call to rugged individualism, but a journey in the company of other disciples who also remember and celebrate Jesus. This remembrance and celebration happen in the telling of the stories about Jesus and the stories he told (the parables) and in the celebration of the eucharist. As one contemporary spiritual writer aptly describes church, "Gather the folks, tell the stories, break the bread."[4]

Discipleship involves becoming compassionate, like the good Samaritan whose actions mirror the actions of God. "Be compassionate as God is compassionate" is the clarion call of Jesus, and it is the defining mark of the followers of Jesus. Compassion is the fruit of the life of the Spirit and the ethics of the community of Jesus, the church. Jesus is the very compassion of God, the one who suffers with his people. "To speak of Jesus as the compassion of God is to reflect on . . . the realization that following Jesus in our times confronts us constantly with human suffering."[5] The church, then, is the assembly of disciples who suffer with their people as Jesus did.

Discipleship, a vision of the Christian life as a journey of transformation, is exemplified in the parables. It leads from life under the dominance of culture to the life of companionship with God through Jesus. The journey includes the stories that provide food and nourishment on the road of life, for they show how important God's reign is in our lives (Mark 4:1–34), how important prayer is in our lives (Luke 11:5–13; 18:1–14), how we need to look at possessions and their role in our lives (Luke 12:13–21; 16:1–13; 16:19–31) and how we need to examine the images for God we have in our lives (Luke 15).

Parables call us into relationship with God and one another. That relationship does not leave us unchanged; rather, it transforms us into more and more compassionate beings, into the likeness of Christ. Telling the story of Jesus as well as our stories is part of discipleship. It involves believing in Jesus, which is much more than believing things about Jesus. In the gospels, "believing in Jesus" does not mean accepting certain doctrines about him. It means to give one's heart to Jesus. It is what the Gospel of Luke describes about Mary, the model disciple, who "treasured all these things in her heart" (Luke 2:51). In the Bible, the term *heart* means one's self at the deepest level. It is a metaphor for the very center and ground of our being. It is what is sometimes described as our heart of hearts, the very core of who we are. The parables are the stories that cause us to have heart-to-heart conversations with God, Jesus and other human beings. After reading, praying and studying the parables we can say, like the two disciples on the road to Emmaus, "Were not our hearts burning within us while he was talking to us on the road, while he was opening the scriptures to us?" (Luke 24:32). Giving one's heart to Jesus means moving from hearing the parables to living them. They will then pulse within us like our hearts and surge through us like our life's blood.

The parables of Jesus will live forever. We will not. While we are alive we need to make the parables our story. In so doing, it will be like meeting the parables of Jesus again for the first time.

For Discussion

1. How does your life story connect with the story of Jesus?

2. How do parables affect the way you live your life?

3. What role does the community of faithful believers, the church, play in your life?

4. How do you practice compassion toward yourself? Toward others?

5. Have you ever had a heart-to-heart conversation with God?

The Stories Jesus Left Behind: Introducing the Parables

"The shortest distance between man and God is through a story."[1]

Everyone loves a good story. I remember my grandfather telling us stories about the old country. How he would come alive and his eye twinkle as he told those stories! My toddler son wants me to tell him stories, not to read them to him out of a book. Some of my friends, especially my rabbi friends, tell stories that kindle my imagination.

Chapter Two

A well-told story enlivens both the listener and the teller. Martin Buber, the Jewish philosopher who wrote the book *I and Thou*, tells a story about the power stories have to move us:

> My grandfather was paralyzed. Once he was asked to tell a story about his teacher and he told how the holy Baal Shem Tov used to jump and dance when he was praying. My grandfather stood up when he was telling the story and the story carried him away so much that he had to jump and dance to show how the master had done it. From that moment, he was healed. This is how stories ought to be told.[2]

Stories are powerful tools for teachers. Jesus, being an excellent storyteller, knew that. In the gospels, especially the synoptic gospels (Matthew, Mark and Luke), Jesus is portrayed as the storyteller of God. Like other rabbis of his day, Jesus used stories as a means of teaching. The gospels are full of the stories he told. One could almost begin a gospel about Jesus with the line, "Once upon a time, in a far off country, there lived a great storyteller." Jesus often employed a type of story called a parable. These are the stories he left for us, to help us wrestle with the meaning of our faith and our lives.

When we speak of the gospel parables, we must remind ourselves that we are not speaking of some kind of teaching device that Jesus used in a vacuum. The language of Jesus' parables comes from his Jewish heritage. Jesus the Jew came from a tradition of marvelous storytellers, as the following story underscores.

> God decided to select a nation to be God's chosen people. First, God interviewed the Greeks. "If I were to be your God and you were to be my people, what could you do for me?" God asked.
>
> "O God," the Greek people replied, "if you were to be our God and we would be your people we would honor you with the finest art and loftiest systems of thought. Our great thinkers would extol you in their writings."
>
> "Thank you for your offer," God said.
>
> Next God visited the Romans. God asked: "If I were to be your God and you were to be my people, what could you do for me?"
>
> "Great ruler of the universe," the Romans said, "we are a nation of builders. If you were to be our God and we were to be your people we would erect great buildings in your name and wonderful road systems so that your people could travel to worship in these great buildings."
>
> God seemed pleased with the offer and thanked the Romans.
>
> From Rome God went all over the world interviewing one nation after another. Finally, God interviewed a Mideastern group, the Jews, who had a reputation for being astute traders. Once again, God asked the question. "If I were to be your God and you were to be my people, what could you do for me?"
>
> "God," the Jewish people said, "we are not known for our power or our art or our buildings. However, we are a nation of storytellers. If you

were to be our God and we were to be your children, we would tell your story throughout the whole world."

God, who also had a reputation for being a wise trader, said: " It's a deal!"[3]

Parables and the Hebrew Scriptures

A major source of Jesus' parables is the Hebrew Scriptures.[4] The earliest biblical parable, found in the Hebrew Scriptures,[5] is Jotham's parable of the trees, told to the people of Shechem in Judges 9:8–15. This parable makes a political statement. Abimelech, the son of the Israelite hero Gideon, sought to become absolute ruler over the Israelites. To eliminate any possible rival, he had the rest of Gideon's sons murdered. Jotham, the only one to survive, tells a story that portrayed Abimeleh as unfit for leadership. It is a story that describes how every tree refused to be king of the trees, except the bramble. The productive olive, fig and vine demurred; the worthless bramble took the throne.

Nathan, David's prophet, uses a parable in 2 Samuel 12 to expose David's killing of Uriah the Hittite after his adulterous affair with Bathsheba, Uriah's wife. This parable is usually called the "parable of the ewe lamb." Nathan used this story to lead David to condemn his own adultery, although David did not realize that Nathan was telling a story about him. David thought he was condemning a thief for stealing a poor man's ewe lamb. It was not until Nathan said, "You are the man!" that David knew he had condemned himself.

The parable also appears in writings that compose the prophetic literature of the Hebrew Bible. Isaiah, Jeremiah and Ezekiel all use it at certain points.

Isaiah 5:1–7 tells a parable about a vineyard to call the people of Judah to recognize their infidelity to God. Judah's only possible answer would be judgment against the vineyard. Judah is asked to pass judgment on itself, much as Nathan's parable to David causes David to pass judgment on himself.

The prophet Ezekiel uses parables at least three times. Ezekiel 16 tells the story of a woman whom God raised alone in the desert. Ezekiel 17 offers the allegory of the eagle, a parable about Judah's failed attempt to make an alliance with Egypt. Ezekiel 23 narrates the parable of the two sisters, Oholah and Oholibah, to tell the story of the unfaithfulness of the kingdom of Israel and the kingdom of Judah to God's covenant prior to the Babylonian exile.

Parables and Hebrew Tradition

If we are to understand the parable as a typical Jewish mode of teaching, we should also look at the parables of the rabbis in the Talmud. Jesus and the gospel writers may have used this source in oral form.

The Hebrew word *Talmud* means "teaching." It is a name applied to a collection of the teachings of the major Jewish rabbis and scholars. These collections existed orally at the time of Jesus and the gospel writers; they were compiled in written form between the years 200 and 500 CE.[6]

In the Talmudic collections, parables are highly esteemed. "So the parable should not be lightly esteemed in your eyes, since by means of the parable a person arrives at the true meaning of the words of the Torah" (*Midrash Song of Songs*, Rabbah I. 1, 8). Rabbinic parables are "simple, secular, mono-episodic, fictional, narrative units that serve to explain the rabbinic understanding of the Torah."[7]

One of the most frequent characters in Talmudic parables is the "king," who usually stands for God. There are 325 "king" parables in the Talmud. Four categories of king parables told by the rabbis in the Talmud bear mention here, as they have obvious parallels in Jesus' parables: 1) the king as the ruler of humankind; 2) the king as a father and Israel as his sons and daughters; 3) the king as a husband and Israel as his wife; 4) the king and his subjects, of whom Israel is his favorite. "King" parables, often patterned on those in the Talmud, are used extensively in the gospel of Matthew, such as the king who gave the great wedding feast in Matthew 21 and the last judgment scene in Matthew 25.

Why did rabbis, both Jesus' contemporaries and those long after him, tell parables? The immediate answer is to interpret the Torah, the first five books of the Hebrew Scriptures. The primary role of the rabbi was to teach (the very title means teacher), so he had to find ways of making difficult scriptural verses come alive. By telling stories, the rabbis could make abstract theological concepts accessible to the people before them. Another reason for telling parables was to explain the relationship between God and Israel. A third was ethical exhortation, to explain the consequences of improper behavior. Finally, the Talmud parables touch on salvation history. By way of parables, the rabbis could explain and interpret God's past actions.

Jesus' Use of Parables

Jesus' parables are found in the gospels. The word *parable* (*parabole*) appears 48 times in the synoptic gospels (17 times in Matthew, 13 in Mark and 18 in Luke). But *parable* is entirely absent from John's gospel and from the rest of the Christian Scriptures as well, except for two uses in Hebrews 9:9 and 11:19

Jesus is a master of the art of telling parables. Like Jotham in the book of Judges and Nathan in 2 Samuel, Jesus uses the parable to challenge his listeners. The parable of the Good Samaritan in Luke 10 and the wicked tenants in Matthew 21:33–41 are good examples. Chapter 9 of Proverbs speaks of Wisdom as a woman preparing a banquet, while in Luke 14:17–24 Jesus tells the parable of the great dinner to which many are invited. Jesus used images from nature: fig trees (Luke 13:6–9), sheep (Luke 15:3–7), farmers sowing seed (Luke 8:4–8). His characters are drawn from daily life: widows (Luke 18:1–8), tax collectors (Luke 18:9–14), soldiers and dishonest servants (Luke 20:9–18). The imagery, characters and situations Jesus used were drawn from his Bible, the Hebrew Scriptures.

Both Jesus' parables and the parables told by other rabbis are drawn from the daily life that common, unsophisticated folk would have felt at home with and understood: a woman kneading yeast into flour (Luke 13:20–21; Matthew 13:33), a dispute between a father and his sons (Luke 15:11–32), a man who has fallen in with robbers (Luke 10:30–35), lost sheep (Luke 15:3–7). Wedding banquets, people on journeys, kings, animals, farming are images chosen both by Jesus and by the rabbis.

Jesus' parables also differ from those of the rabbis. His are often more nuanced and developed in plot and character. The rabbis generally told parables to illustrate the meaning of a particular Torah text. Jesus did this, but he also made more creative use of his parables. They were often open-ended, allowing for more than one interpretation by his listeners. We can understand Jesus' parables on many different levels. For example, it is possible to read the parable of the talents (Matthew 25:14–30) as a story about final judgment; it also could be about the right use of one's earthly goods.

In brief, parables were a means by which Jesus taught the word of God. What occasions, what life-situations prompted Jesus to tell a parable? It is possible to delineate two settings for Jesus' parables. One is Jesus preaching to the crowds or to the disciples; these were often the settings for telling the kingdom parables. A second setting for the parables is in Jesus' debates with the Pharisees and Sadducees.

The simplest of parables is the proverb. Jesus often used these short sayings of comparison, which draw from ordinary experience to illustrate how life should be lived. Matthew's Sermon on the Mount provides a couple of examples of Jesus' use of proverbs. "You are the salt of the earth" (Matthew 5:13); "You are the light of the world. A city built on a hill cannot be hid" (Matthew 5:14).

What Is a Parable?

Behind our English word *parable* stands the Greek noun *parabole*, which is derived from the preposition *para*, meaning "alongside of," and the verb *ballein*, meaning "to cast, to place or to throw." Etymologically, the term *parable* means that one thing is understood in juxtaposition or comparison with another. A parable, then, intends to throw some meaning alongside of the story.

When Jesus taught with parables, he illustrated ideas about the kingdom of God by examples ("thrown beside") drawn from everyday experiences of his listeners. He would begin thusly: "The kingdom of God is like . . ." a fig tree, a pearl, a sower, a mustard seed, a king who goes on a journey. Parables recount a common incident from daily life in concise, figurative form to illustrate a spiritual truth. Just like the ancients, we look for the meaning alongside the story. A parable is intended to challenge the listener's values and way of looking at life and bring about a change of heart. Parables use the familiar to explain the unfamiliar. Put very simply, a parable is simply a story with religious meaning drawn from ordinary life, or a story with a moral.

Parables as Text

The parables we experience come to us as a text in the gospels, not as the spoken stories they were originally. This means that we cannot get back to the raw experience behind the text, but only to the text itself as preserved by the gospel writers. Nor can we get back to the reaction of the first audience to the story. Biblical scholars point out that it is unlikely that each of the parables in the gospels was actually told by the historical Jesus. Mark, Matthew and Luke reworked stories from the oral tradition. The written parables are the early church's memories and interpretations of the historical Jesus' parables.

A parable engages the listener in dialogue. In our case, because neither the speaker (Jesus) nor the recorder (the particular gospel writer) is visibly present, we have to dialogue with the text. This means we need to read the text carefully.

Types of Parables

Biblical scholars distinguish three types of parables. Some are about ordinary events that all people have experienced in one way or another, such as the widow's search for the lost coin (Luke 15:8–10). The kingdom of God is compared to these common experiences. Others, such as the story of the sower who went out to sow seed (Luke 8:5–8), tell a simple story created by Jesus to illustrate a point about the kingdom. A third kind, such as the parable of the Good Samaritan (Luke 10:30–37), illustrates the way people live in the kingdom.

Biblical scholars disagree on the exact number and particular names of parables in the gospels. For convenience, the list from the *New Interpreter's Bible* is included here.

Parables in the synoptic gospels[8]

PARBLES TITLE	LUKE	MATTHEW	MARK
Patches and wineskins[1]	5:36–39	9:16–17	2:21–22
The blind leading the blind[2]	6:39–40	15:14b	
The log in your own eye[2]	6:41–42	7:3–4	
Producing good fruit[2]	6:43–45	7:16–20	
The two builders/building on a solid foundation	6:46–49	7:24–27	
The riddle of the children	7:31–35	11:16–19	
The two debtors	7:41–43		
The lamp	8:16	5:14–16	4:21–22
Seed and the soil/the sower	8:4–8	13:3–8	4:3–9
The good Samaritan	10:30–35		
The parable of a shameless neighbor	11:5–8		
The kingdom divided against itself[3]	11:17a	12:25a	3:25

TITLE	LUKE	MATTHEW	MARK
The house divided against itself[3]	11:17b	12:25b	3:25
The return of the unclean spirit	11:24–26	12:43–45	
The rich fool	12:16–21		
The returning master	12:36–38		
The thief in the night/the watchful owner	12:39–40	24:43–44	
The good and wicked servants	12:42–46	24:45–51	13:33–37
Going before a judge	12:58–59	5:25–26	
The barren fig tree	13:6–9	21:20–22	11:20–25
The mustard seed	13:18–19	13:31–32	4:30–32
The yeast	13:20–21	13:33	
The narrow door	13:24–30		
The choice of places at table	14:7–11		
The great supper/great banquet	14:16–24	22:1–14	
The fool at work	14:28–30		
The fool at war	14:31–32		
The lost sheep	15:3–7	18:12–14	
The lost coin	15:8–10		
The prodigal son	15:11–32		
The dishonest steward	16:1–9		
The rich man and Lazarus	16:19–31		
The servant who serves without reward	17:7–10		
The unjust judge and the persistent widow	18:1–8		
The Pharisee and the tax collector	18:9–14		
The talents/the greedy and vengeful king	19:11–27	25:14–30	
The wicked tenants/the Lord's vineyard given to others/vineyard tenants	20:9–18	21:33–44	12:1–11
The fig tree in bloom[1]	21:29–31	24:32–35	13:28–29
The weeds		13:24–30	
The hidden treasure and the pearl		13:44–46	
The net		13:47–48	
The owner of a house		13:52	
What can defile[4]	15:10–11		7:14–15
The unmerciful servant		18:23–35	
The laborers in the vineyard		20:1–16	
The two sons		21:28–32	
The bridesmaids		25:1–13	
The seed growing of itself			4:26–29
The watchful servants			13:33–37

1 Although treated as a saying in Matthew and Mark, this passage is described as a parable by Luke.

2 Although treated as a saying in Matthew, this passage is described as a parable by Luke.

3 Although treated as a saying in Matthew and Luke, this passage is described as a parable by Mark.

4 This passage is described as a parable by both Matthew (15:15) and Mark (7:17).

In a sense, the parables are two parts of a conversation: Jesus' part and the gospel writer's part. We know that the words we read reflect the actual sayings of Jesus as interpreted and applied by the particular gospel's community. The reader then reacts to the parable he or she has read. But to do so, we must know something of the structure of a parable and of its context: the time, place and situation in which the evangelist wrote his words down, and for whom he wrote them.

By the time the memories of Jesus' words were written down, the circumstances of the lives of his followers had changed. These changes influenced the way they remembered and understood the parables. Biblical scholars list many factors that need to be taken into account. Some of the more important of these are listed below:

- The parables were translated from the original Aramaic, which Jesus spoke, into Greek, the language in which the gospels were written, causing subtle changes in meaning. In turn, the gospels were later translated into Latin and then into modern languages.

- As happens in ordinary conversation, the parables were often embellished as they were retold. By the time they were written down, the embellishments had been included.

- Parables originally addressed to the opponents of Jesus or to the crowds who followed him were, in many cases, applied by the primitive church to the actual situation of the Christian community of a later day.

How to Read the Parables as Narrative

After reading a parable, preferably aloud, from more than one modern, reputable English translation of the Bible, the reader should read both the notes on the parable and, if there is one, the parallel to the parable from another gospel. While doing this, ask the following:

- To whom is Jesus speaking?

- What is the topic or central point of the parable?

- With which person or event in the story does the reader identify?

- What lesson is drawn from this comparison?

- How is the reader being asked to change as a result of hearing or reading the parable?

When we look at the parables in the gospels, we are looking at narratives. They are short stories or, more precisely, teaching stories. Stylistically, as pieces of literature, the parables are characterized by the following:

- There is a narrator or storyteller: Jesus.

- The narration is concise—only the necessary people appear and much information is communicated by suggestion. In the parable of the prodigal son, for example, we have only a suggestion of how large the inheritance was that the younger son asked for (see Luke 15).

- Groups of people tend to be treated as single characters. In the prodigal son, the younger of the two boys represents sinners seeking reconciliation with God, while the father represents God (see Luke 15:11–21).

- Usually only two characters interact at the same time. Only the father and the younger son interact at first. Later only the father and the older son interact (see Luke 15:11–21).

- The listener is asked to focus on only one perspective at a time. In the story of the prodigal son, the listener is asked to focus at first only on the perspective of the younger son and father; later on, the listener is asked to focus on the perspective of the older son and the father (see Luke 15).

In terms of character portrayal, the following apply to parables:

- There is little description in terms of attributes, feelings or emotions; what people do indicates their characters. So what the younger boy does in the parable of the prodigal son is important: at first he squanders the inheritance, then he seeks forgiveness and reunification. We don't know the emotions (see Luke 15:11–21).

- Motivations are rarely given. We have no clear, explicit motive for why the younger son wanted to grab his inheritance and leave home (see Luke 15:11–21).

- Secondary characters are not described in any detail. Such is the case with the servants who kill the fatted calf in the story of the prodigal son (see Luke 15:11–21).

Certain plot devices are also present:

- Repetition is the way the action is maintained. In the parable of the prodigal son, the two sons come home with two different agendas (see Luke 15).

- The parable's final verse(s) often contain the moral of the story. In the case of the prodigal son, "He was lost and has been found!" (Luke 15:32).

- There is a lack of conclusion and certain issues are left unresolved. The unresolved issue in the parable of the prodigal son is where the older son stands in relationship to the father? Does he reconcile? The reader is simply left dangling.

The Parables in Context

One big complaint that people have with journalists is that they often quote others out of context. The biggest complaint biblical scholars have with people who read the parables is that they often don't see them in their proper context, that is, the context of the gospel in which they appear.

Jesus' parables existed first in the *social* context of his ministry and the *religious* context of his mission and proclamation. But a parable also exists in a *literary* context—it appears in a certain section of a particular gospel. In a sense, the original context of the parables is irretrievable, since we can never be in the historical position of Jesus' audience. The original context is always a reconstruction, and this reconstruction requires a whole series of judgments about the life and ministry of Jesus on the part of the interpreter.

In reflecting on a parable, we have to take into account both the context in which Jesus told it and the literary context in which the gospel writer wrote it if we are to hear the challenge it has for us. Let us take an example from the gospel of Luke. Luke was recording the parables not as a Jew hearing them from the lips of Jesus, but as a Christian who had talked about and reflected on these stories with other believers.

For example, Luke wrote a parable that Jesus told about a man who gave a feast to which the invited guests did not come (Luke 16:1–24). The story follows the accepted etiquette of the time. First the guests received a preparatory invitation, which did not give the exact time of the banquet. Then, when all was ready, the host would send his servants with a second invitation to those who had been invited. Courtesy demanded that those who had been invited (and who had presumably accepted) should attend. Not to do so was a great offense.

The host is understandably angry when the invited guests all give excuses for not being able to attend. Now comes the twist. The host decides to invite the poor from the city streets. Even so, there is still room, so he sends out his servants a second time into the country lanes where foreigners and outcasts live, telling them to bring in all they can find. Thus, the poor, the outcasts and the homeless are compelled to come to the banquet.

The historical Jesus told this story as a rebuke of the critics who refused to listen to him. By the time Luke wrote this parable, that was not a big problem for his community. Luke's community was composed of those who had accepted the invitation. Those who had been first invited in the parable represent the Jews who had not accepted Christ. Therefore, Luke uses the parable as a missionary statement indicating that all kinds of people are called to the kingdom. We can see a reference to this intention in the two calls. The first sending forth of the servants was a call to the tax collectors and sinners in Israel; the second, which came at a later time, sent forth the call to the Gentiles.

This is an example of *contextual* reading of a parable. All parables in the gospels need to be read this way.

An Overview of the Parables in the Synoptic Gospels

The social setting of the parables reflects the first-century Mediterranean experience of a largely agrarian society. Such an audience would recognize the economic implications of losing a sheep (Matthew 18:12–24) and the social shame endured by a father whose wayward son runs off and squanders his inheritance (Luke 15:11–32). They would know how unthinkable it would be to slight the honor of a king by refusing his invitation to dinner (Matthew 22:1–14) and how dangerous the road from Jerusalem to Jericho was for a man traveling alone—at the mercy of strangers who turned out to be thieves (Luke 10:29–37).

Some parables are common to all three synoptics (see chart on page 16), such as the sower who went out to sow seed (Mark 4:1–12; Matthew 13:1–9; Luke 8:4–10), describing four possible responses to hearing the message of Jesus. The paradoxical story of tenants who resist the master's servants and kill his son is also a shared synoptic tradition (Mark 12:1–11; Matthew 21:33–46; Luke 20:9–19). It reflects an intense atmosphere of hostility between the Christian and Jewish communities. The great feast or wedding banquet to which many were invited and some refused (Luke 14:16–24; Matthew 22:2–10) also reflects the hostility between Jewish and Christian groups struggling for survival after the destruction of Jerusalem in 70 CE.

Some parables are unique to the gospel of Luke; it has the largest number. Luke alone preserves the story of the good Samaritan (10:29–37), a commentary on the nature of neighborly compassion. The dramatic scene contrasting the Pharisee and the tax collector (18:9–14) is quite a reversal parable. The tax collector is acceptable to God, not because of his performance or status but because he is receptive and vulnerable before God. The story of the widow who is so desperate for the financial settlement of her estate that she pesters an unwilling judge and is persistent to the point that the judge fears she will strike him (Luke 18:1–8) is preserved only in Luke's gospel as well. Luke alone narrates the story of the woman who searches the house for the lost coin (Luke 15:8–10), the prodigal son (Luke 15:11–32) and many others.

While it is true that men and male activities dominate the parables, women are also models for the true character of God. Their actions portray what the reign of God really means. The yeast a woman kneads into dough makes everyone in the community rise and thus become capable of satisfying the hunger of others (Matthew 13:33; Luke 13:20–21). The woman in this parable is also a representation of God, as is the woman who searches the house for the one missing coin (Luke 15:8–10). A woman's world of ten lamp-carrying bridesmaids (Matthew 25:10–13) is offered as metaphoric parallel to the story of the three male servants given talents (Matthew 25:14–30).

By means of parables, Jesus attempted to convey the true nature of a loving and benevolent God. God is like a merchant who sells everything in order to possess the single pearl, a people dearly loved and cherished (Matthew 13:44–46). God is like a shepherd who rejoices in finding the stray and doesn't punish it for wandering off (Matthew 18:12–14). God is like the forgiving father figure in the parable of the prodigal son (Luke 15:11–32).

As a sign of hope for a struggling community, Jesus' parables assure believers that the future of the reign of God is inevitable. The seed in the earth has a life of its own (Mark 4:26–29). A tiny mustard seed grows from insignificance to a supportive bush that welcomes all the birds of the air (Mark 4:30–32). The worrisome and threatening presence of evil in the midst of good is explained by the farmer's wisdom, which allows weeds and wheat to grow together until harvest (Matthew 13).

Parables reinforce Jesus' teachings on care for the poor and on forgiveness. For example, the story of the rich man who refuses to pay attention to Lazarus, the poor man at his door, states important values for the community: attention to the poor rather than avoidance of them, justice to those right at one's door and sharing wealth with the needy (Luke 16:19–31).

The Power of Stories

Nobel laureate Elie Wiesel drives home the power of stories.

When the great rabbi Baal Shem Tov saw misfortune threatening the Jews, it was his custom to go into a certain part of the forest to meditate. There he would light a fire, say a special prayer and the miracle would be accomplished and misfortune averted.

Later, when his disciple, the celebrated Magid of Mezeritch, had occasion for the same reason to intercede with heaven, he would go to the same place in the forest and say: "Master of the Universe, listen! I do not know how to light the fire, but I am still able to say the prayer." And again, the miracle would be accomplished.

Still later, Rabbi Moshe-Leib of Sassov, in order to save his people once more, would go into the forest and say: "I do not know how to light the fire. I do not know the prayer. But I know the place and this must be sufficient." It was sufficient and the miracle was accomplished.

Then it fell to rabbi Israel of Rizhin to overcome misfortune. Sitting in his armchair, his head in his hands, he spoke to God: "I cannot even find the place in the forest. All I can do is tell the story and this must be sufficient." And it was sufficient.

God made [us] because he loves stories.[9]

Wiesel's tale illustrates the power of stories even when the details of their original context are lost. This is the situation we face when trying to retrieve the original settings and meanings of Jesus' parables. The form in which they have come to us is now centuries removed from their first telling. Like Rabbi Israel of Rizhin, all we have is the story. This is the heritage Jesus and the gospel writers left us.

Points for Reflection

In his parables, Jesus always began with the familiar. Jesus told how God is encountered in sowing and reaping (Mark 4:1–9), in weeding and harvesting (Matthew 13:24–30), in baking bread (Matthew 13:33) and in searching for what is lost (Luke 15:1–32). In the same way, an effective reader of the parables today transforms the gospel images and situations into ones that relate to his or her everyday world. This is an overwhelming challenge even for the best reader.

Jesus' parables, as recorded in the gospels, do not stay on the level of the predictable. Parables were not meant to be pleasant stories that entertained people, like jokes, or that confirmed the status quo. Parables are not a joking matter. They were startling and confusing, usually having an unexpected twist that left the hearers pondering what the story meant and what it demanded.

Parables leave today's reader in a similar mood. For example, in the parable of the woman who searches her house for a lost coin (Luke 15:8–10), the theme of God searching for the lost sinner transcends all ages and applies to people today, just as in Jesus' day. Or the parable of the Pharisee and the tax collector (Luke 18:9–14), which deals with prayer, is still valid today, for prayer is just as meaningful an experience for people now as it was in Jesus' time.

Jesus' parables are invitations to see the activity of God as God sees it, and to act as Jesus acted. Such a vision demands profound changes in the way the reader or listener thinks about God and the presence of God, both as it can be in the here and now and in the future. By shattering the accepted structures of our world, parables remove our defenses and make us vulnerable to God. They never reinforce life as it is; the gospel is always about change, after all. An effective reader prays with and studies the text of a parable so as to understand what it originally meant and then tries, as best he or she can, to see how that unsettling dynamic is active in his or her life.

People should feel uncomfortable after reading or hearing a parable and, at the same time, be challenged to change their lives. The aim of parables is to convert the listener. "Jesus' parables affected those who heard them and they are supposed to affect us. They are intended to stun us into reevaluating our positions, our enemies, our love and practice of justice."[10] Parables challenge people in their heart of hearts, so that they will be moved to praise God and to transformative action.

The parables can teach us how to live life. The parables of Jesus are short and to the point. Parables always side with the marginal and the disenfranchised: widows, a victim of robbers, the poor. They proclaim that God is not neutral. Rather, God is always on the side of those who are poorest and most oppressed. This is shown, for example, in the parables of the rich man and Lazarus (Luke 16:19–31), the rich fool (Luke 12:16–21) and the prodigal son (Luke 15:11–32).

The gospel parables do not call us to privatism. Biblical religion is always an affair of the community. From its inception, for the gospel writers, the people of God is a community bound together by the covenant. But Jesus' parables put another spin on the vision of a covenant community. In the story of the great feast (Luke 14:15–24), for example, the people of God encompasses all, particularly the despised and outcast. Jesus' parable of the workers in the vineyard (Matthew

20:1–16) offers an entirely disconcerting and unsettling vision of a just community. The scenario is not of each one pulling his or her own weight with appropriate compensation. Rather, the parable presents the believing community, the church, as one in which each member has the means by which to subsist, no matter what his or her contribution is to the group. In this parable, God is presented as the gracious employer who contradicts all contemporary notions of a just employer.[11]

The power of Jesus' storytelling came from his whole life being a parable. His way of living and embracing the cross was a witness to the very presence of God. Jesus was a public witness, and the Greek word for witness is *martyr!* Likewise, all who encounter both Jesus, the parable of God and his parables in our own day are called to give such personal witness. The Christian's life needs to be a lived parable. No faith life takes place unless the life of the Christian is a living witness to faith. Followers of Jesus, like Jesus himself, have a story to tell. The challenge is to connect the individual stories of faith with the story of Jesus and the community's story. We all need to remember that our story is what Jeremiah called "a burning fire shut up in my bones" (Jeremiah 20:9).

The gospel parables provide tales for our spiritual pilgrimage. They are not only the stories that Jesus left behind; they are the stories we still learn as we grow, like the young Jesus, in wisdom and knowledge and grace before God and humankind (see Luke 2:52). They are the stories we share at the celebration of the eucharist. Like the disciples on the road to Emmaus we ask, "Were not our hearts burning within us?" (Luke 24:32). "The purpose of the scripture is to burn the heart. Once the heart burns, the eyes are opened to see the spiritual dimension of what is taking place."[12]

For Discussion

1. What role do stories play in your life? In your family? In your practice of faith?

2. Why do you think Jesus used parables?

3. Do you have a favorite parable of Jesus? Which one? Why is it your favorite?

4. As a result of reading this chapter, do you have a better idea of how to read a gospel parable? Explain.

5. What does it mean to say that a Christian's life needs to be a lived parable?

Mark's Parables of the Kingdom

"He began to teach them many things
in parables."

(Mark 4:2)

Before exploring some of the parables in the gospel of
Mark, some background is in order. Like all the gospels,
Mark is a popular work intended to evoke faith that Jesus is the
Messiah and Son of God (Mark 1:1). One way to read Mark is as
what is technically called a *folktale*, a realistic narrative with particu-
larizing detail that is meant to be read aloud to hearers, much as a
story would be told. Where this popular story originated is one of
the great puzzles of biblical scholarship.[1]

Complex factors led to the writing of the gospels in the second half of the first century. The expected return of Jesus in glory was delayed and the eyewitnesses of his ministry were dying or being martyred in the first organized persecutions of Christians. For the church there was increasing need for a standardized version of Jesus' life and teachings both to answer questions of authority and to serve as a missionary tool in the evangelization of the Gentiles. The gospels were written to answer these needs.

The gospel of Mark, the earliest of the four, was written between 65 and 75 CE. Most scholars think it was composed before the destruction of the Temple of Jerusalem in 70 CE, since its destruction does not seem to be reflected in the gospel. Toward the end of the Emperor Nero's reign (54–68 CE), Christians in Rome suffered terrible persecutions. Apocalyptic expectations surged with the Jewish War of 66–70 CE. Both of these facts are reflected in Mark, which seems to have been written for a church undergoing persecution. The most ancient church traditions associate the gospel of Mark with the apostle Peter and the city of Rome. Eusebius's *Ecclesiastical History* (3.39) quotes Papias (ca. 140 CE), who notes that Mark was "Peter's interpreter." Although the Greek and Latin fathers up to St. Jerome in the fifth century associate Mark's gospel with Peter, modern biblical scholars doubt the connection.

However, modern biblical scholarship supports Rome as the location of the writing of the gospel of Mark. The fact that Mark explains both Jewish customs and Aramaic expressions suggests a primarily Gentile audience.[2] Mark contains many words borrowed from Latin, which would support a Roman location, except that most of the loan words are military terms and, therefore, might have come from any place in the Empire. That Matthew and Luke both used Mark in writing their gospels suggests that it came from a well-known Christian center.

Mark's community, then, was predominantly but not exclusively Gentile. They did not observe Mosaic law and had known or were about to experience persecution. This accounts for the heavily apocalyptic tone of the work. As one study guide for Mark notes, theologically and pastorally, Mark retells the Jesus story to show that the kingdom in its glory comes at the end of a path of suffering and service.[3] As is the case with all of the gospels, the writer is unknown, but he wrote in vernacular Greek *(Koine)* from a location important enough that his gospel was well known and foundational for the writing of subsequent gospels.

Kingdom Vocabulary

Before proceeding to look at the various parables about the kingdom contained in the gospels, it is important to reflect on the gospel use of the term "kingdom of God." The synoptic gospels make extensive use of the Greek phrase *basileia tou theou*. Historically, this phrase has most often been translated as the "kingdom of God." It is found 14 times in the gospel of Mark and 32 times in the gospel of Luke; Matthew uses either "kingdom of Heaven" or "kingdom of God" 38 times. It rarely appears in other books of the Christian Scriptures. It is mentioned in John 3:3, 5 and is used six times in the Acts of the Apostles.

All three of the synoptic gospels have "kingdom" parables. The "kingdom" designates the central theme of the mission of Jesus. The phrase *basileia tou theou* is rich in meaning; it is difficult to find an adequate phrase in English for the Greek that accurately conveys all the nuances of its meaning.

Translating *basileia tou theou* as "kingdom of God" is problematic, first because it conveys the notion of a geographical locale with fixed boundaries. It has long been recognized in general and in the world of biblical scholarship that God's *basileia* signifies a divine rule, not a "kingdom" in a territorial or political sense.

In addition, the term kingdom *(basileia)* in a first-century Palestinian context would first call to mind the Roman imperial system of domination and exploitation. Jesus' proclamation of the *basileia* of God offered an alternative vision to that of the empire of Rome. The *basileia* that Jesus announced was one in which there was no more victimization or domination. The beginning of the *basileia* was already present incipiently in Jesus' healing and liberating practices, the inclusive table-sharing of his followers and their domination-free relationships. The political threat that such a subversive vision presented to the Roman imperial system is clear from the crucifixion of Jesus. He was crucified as a criminal whom the Roman authorities thought was attempting to establish his own political kingdom in opposition to Rome.

A further difficulty with the translation "kingdom of God" is that it presents an image of God as king, reinforcing a male, monarchical and hierarchical model of God's rule. For communities of believers whose experience of governance is democratic, who have become conscious of the limitations and dangers of human rulers who claim divine status or appointment (as kings did in the ancient world) and who have become conscious of the limitations and dangers of solely male images of God, "kingdom" is an inadequate term.

If the *basileia tou theou* is translated as the "reign of God," this is an improvement. While the word *reign* has historical echoes of government, of nations ruled by kings, of a wealthy aristocratic class, of a large poor peasant class, of warring countries and of hierarchy that deals in laws, relations and economics, hereditary and land rights, it nonetheless can be broadened.

The word *reign* is also related to the word *rein:* a discipline, a hold, a check that controls, a way of being in life. These *reins,* like those used with a horse, stop, slow down, give direction and alter paths. The *reign* of God operates like *reins* on the world, on evil, on circumstances and on people, especially those who accept the *rein* as part of belonging to the faith community that follows the teachings of Jesus. While translating the phrase "kingdom of God" as "reign of God" does not solve or address all translation issues, it does offer an alternative view more closely akin to the gospel usage in the parables.

Recognizing that no phrase adequately captures all that *basileia tou theou* signifies, alternative translations of *basileia* include *kingdom, rule, reign, rein, realm, empire, domain, presence* and *commonweal*. With adequate explanation, some contemporary scholars and writers leave it untranslated, as *basileia*. While none of these terms is perfect, it is helpful for any reader or interpreter of the parables of the *basileia tou theou* to experiment with new phrases to jolt one's consciousness into wrestling with the meaning of the phrase.

Whatever translation one adopts, it is important that it convey a sense of God's saving mercy over all of creation, inaugurated with the incarnation and ministry of Jesus. The *basileia* is continued in the faithful ministry of the believing community, the church, but not yet fully manifested. It is not gender specific, patriarchal or a fixed place located in the beyond. Nor is it the same as the church. It is the authoritative saving mercy of God and the freedom made possible by God-with-us.

Since this book quotes the parables from the *New Revised Standard Version* of the Bible and the publishers of this version rightly demand that the text not be changed, the phrase "kingdom of God" is used in the cited and quoted parables. However, in both interpreting and commenting on these parables, every attempt will be made whenever possible to use alternative, inclusive vocabulary that eliminates the concept of domination to convey the rich meaning of the *basileia tou theou*.

Parables in the Gospel of Mark

Mark's gospel contains many small discourses. In one of these, Jesus teaches in parables, and it sets the stage for the rest of his teachings in the gospel. In fact, in his portrayals of Jesus, Mark uses the noun *teaching (didache)* five times and the corresponding verb *to teach (didacho)* seventeen times.

As a teacher, Jesus must have spoken directly as well as in stories and sayings. But the gospels do not present these conversations or discourses word-for-word. The gospels were written *after* the resurrection with the intention of responding to new issues and problems in the Christian communities.

The parables are also literary devices. The evangelists composed the "literary discourses" in the gospels. Parables are key elements in those discourses.

There is a difference, then, between an *historical* discourse, which marks a historical moment, and a *literary* discourse, which refers to the same moment in literature. Historically, a discourse was delivered in one place, at one time and for one particular audience. *Literarily*, however, an author could rise above the historical context. A discourse could start in one place and at a particular time and then, with little or no transition, jump to another place and time, able to speak with a new voice for new people confronting challenges of their own. This situation is the case with the parable of the sower (Mark 4:1–34). The beginning of the discourse is simple. According to the introduction, Jesus spoke to a large crowd by the sea and he spoke to them in parables (Mark 4:1–2).

The discourse, then, presents one of the many parables Jesus told the crowd, that of the sower (Mark 4:3–9). At this point, the audience changes with the stroke of a pen; the crowd disappears, and Jesus is alone with those who were around him along with the twelve (Mark 4:10a). His message to them unfolds in three parts: 1) he explains why he spoke in parables (Mark 4:10–12); 2) he interprets for them the parable of the sower (Mark 4:13–20); 3) he concludes by speaking further about parables and their purpose (Mark 4:21–25).

The discourse then returns to its original audience, and Jesus presents two further parables to the *crowd*, both of which concern the kingdom of God (Mark 4:26–32). The discourse ends by reaffirming the distinction between Jesus' teaching to the *crowds*, which was done with many such parables, and his teachings to his own *disciples*, which included private explanations (Mark 4:33–34).

In Mark's literary discourse, Jesus has distinct audiences: the crowd (4:1), those who were around him with the twelve (4:10) and his own disciples (4:34). In the narrator's introduction (Mark 4:1–2) and the conclusion (Mark 4:33–34), as well as in Jesus' message to his own disciples (Mark 4:10–12), the gospel says that Jesus addressed the audiences differently. He spoke *publicly* to the crowds in parables, but he explained the parables *privately* only to his disciples, that is, to those who were around him along with the twelve.

Using these distinctions, we can show how Mark has built a bridge between the historical time of Jesus, when the parables were quite clear, and the evangelist's own time, when they required some explanation. Once explained, the parables again became clear, but only for those who gathered around Jesus.

The discourse includes yet another important distinction between those who "were around Jesus" (Mark 4:7–10; Mark 3:32) with the twelve and those who were *outside* (Mark 4:11; 3:32). For those *outside*, not only do the parables remain obscure, but also no explanation will suffice to clarify them (Mark 4:12). To understand the parables according to the gospel of Mark, you have to be an intimate follower of Jesus and associated with the twelve in the new Israel, which is a synonym for the church. You have to be part of the inner group.

Teaching in Parables

"Teaching in parables" usually implies that several parables were presented. The gospel of Mark states that Jesus spoke with many parables on this occasion (Mark 4:33). At this point, however, only one of those parables is retold: the sower and the seed.

> [3]"Listen! A sower went out to sow. [4]And as he sowed, some seed fell on the path, and the birds came and ate it up. [5]Other seed fell on rocky ground, where it did not have much soil, and it sprang up quickly, since it had no depth of soil. [6]And when the sun rose, it was scorched; and since it had no root, it withered away. [7]Other seed fell among thorns, and the thorns grew up and choked it, and it yielded no grain. [8]Other seed fell into good soil and brought forth grain, growing up and increasing and yielding thirty and sixty and a hundredfold." [9]And he said, "Let anyone with ears to hear listen!" (Mark 4:3–9)

To get the crowd's full attention, Jesus gives the parable a one-word preface: "Listen!" Then he launches into "A sower went out to sow" (Mark 4:3). Notice the use of the imperative. Jesus' first word of the parable in verse 3, "Listen!" is echoed in his final exhortation in verse 9, "Let anyone with ears to hear listen!" This is then commented on in verse 12 in words quoted from Isaiah 6:10 to the effect that the people "listen and listen, yet understand nothing." The language attributed to Jesus indicates the authority with which he is said to have spoken. Furthermore, it might well have evoked in the minds of Mark's readers the command to hear, and therefore to obey, the demands of the speaker. The parable could easily have focused on the sower and the act of sowing, but it does not. These merely provide a literary setting for the seed, the kinds of ground on which it fell and what subsequently happened to it (Mark 4:4–8). The parable focuses mostly on the soil: the path, the rocky ground, the thorns and the rich soil. The seed is the same in each case. What differs is the soil. What happens to the seed depends entirely on the quality of the soil where it falls.

The parable is a challenge to Jesus' listeners, inviting each to reflect on how he or she is responding to Jesus' ministry, measuring their response against the

idea of the rich soil that yields an abundant harvest of fruit. The message of the parable is primarily one of encouragement.

The symbolism of bearing fruit is common in both the Hebrew Scriptures and the teaching of Jesus. Jesus used the parable to confront the people with God's demand for obedience to his will. The contrast between fruitful and barren soils represents the contrast between those who are responsive to God's commands and, therefore, true members of his people and those who fail to obey his will. It is those who are responsive and obedient to God's will who belong to God's realm.

In summation, "hearing" Jesus, according to the parable in the gospel of Mark, is not simply the physical act, but more the moral action of response and obedience to him and to his teachings. The first parable of chapter 4 is a good introduction to the remainder of the discourse, which centers on the problem of truly hearing and understanding the parables.

The Purpose of the Parables According to Mark

[10]When he was alone, those who were around him along with the twelve asked him about the parables. [11]And he said to them, "To you has been given the secret of the kingdom of God, but for those outside, everything comes in parables; [12]in order that
'they may indeed look, but not perceive,
and may indeed listen, but not understand;
so that they may not turn again
and be forgiven.'" (Mark 4:10–12)

After the parable of the sower and Jesus' challenge to hear (Mark 4:3–9), the crowd disappears. Jesus is left alone with the twelve, who question him about the parables. Jesus explains why they were able to understand while those outside were not. Those with the twelve have been granted the secret of the realm of God (Mark 1:14–15). As part of the new Israel, the church, open to Jew and Gentile, they have the experience that allows them to understand. What was hidden in the past, and even now is hidden from others, God has revealed to them.

Those who remain outside have not received the mystery of the realm of God, whereby all human beings are called to participate in the new Israel, the church. For them, Jesus' teaching in parables remains opaque. They lack the experience of faith and commitment that would allow them to understand. As a result, the purpose of the parables ends up being exactly the opposite of what Jesus meant them to be. What should bring perception and understanding does not. This is marvelously expressed by an adaptation of Isaiah 6:9–10, where God says the same thing to Isaiah about the people of Israel.

> [13]And he said to them, "Do you not understand this parable? Then how will you understand all the parables? [14]The sower sows the word. [15]These are the ones on the path where the word is sown: when they hear, Satan immediately comes and takes away the word that is sown in them. [16]And these are the ones sown on rocky ground: when they hear the word, they immediately receive it with joy. [17]But they have no root, and endure only for a while; then, when trouble or persecution arises on account of the word, immediately they fall away. [18]And others are those sown among the thorns: these are the ones who hear the word, [19]but the cares of the world and the lure of wealth, and the desire for other things come in and choke the word, and it yields nothing. [20]And these are the ones sown on the good soil; they hear the word and accept it and bear fruit, thirty and sixty and a hundredfold." (Mark 4:13–20)

After explaining the purpose of the parables, Jesus interprets the one parable presented while he was addressing the whole crowd (Mark 4:3). If the disciples do not understand this parable, how can any of the others (Mark 4:13)? The parable of the sower and the seed was not selected at random. This parable provides the key for understanding all the others.

In his interpretation, Jesus identifies the seed as the word of God, which Jesus sows by telling the parable. He then shows what happened to the word that fell on the path, on rocky ground, among the thorns and on rich soil. In the first *telling* of the parable (Mark 4:3–9), emphasis lay on the *seed* and what happened to it, here emphasis is placed on the *word*.

In the *interpretation*, Jesus shifts the emphasis from the seed to the various kinds of ground. The ground is the metaphor for disciples. He mentions again the rich ground, the climax of the first telling and the ideal against which one can measure oneself, but without additional development. The other kinds of ground, and what happened to seeds that fell on them, receive a new and imaginative treatment by Jesus.

Jesus' interpretation maintains that there are different types of disciples in whom the word is sown:

- The *path*, from whom the word is immediately snatched away by Satan, are disciples who hardly even hear the word.

- The *rocky ground*, in whom the word is joyfully received but has no roots are those disciples who hear the word but fall away when tribulation or persecution comes because of the word.

- The *thorns*, in whom the word is choked by worldly anxiety, the lure of riches or craving for other things, hear the word but bear no fruit.

- The *rich soil* represents disciples who not only hear the word but accept it and bear fruit thirty and sixty and hundredfold.

The first telling of the parable held up an ideal. The second interpretation aimed at formation. In presenting it, Mark may have meant to evoke the disciples' baptismal commitment. This interpretation is suggested by two themes, the sowing of the word and the bearing of fruit. As he evoked the baptismal commitment, Mark also held up the challenges faced by the early Christians, including his readers, who experienced tribulation, persecution, worldly anxiety and the lure of riches and other cravings.

Jesus closes the story with an amazing statement: Good soil yields not only fruit but thirty and sixty and a hundred times what was sown! These are astounding crops! His first hearers would have known that. The seeds of God's realm sown in a receptive heart grow and multiply far beyond ordinary expectations. It is the nature of the kingdom to produce such results, that is, enormous harvests!

Points for Reflection

If we long for results like this in our own discipleship experiences, we can cooperate with the divine sower by softening our hearts, by opening our good soil to the seeds already sown there. Then by the grace of God and with our active cooperation, our spiritual crops will spill their wealth into every corner of our lives and into the lives of those around us.

In this parable of the sower, Jesus challenges us: If you have ears, hear this! He does not refer to our physical ears, but to the power of the heart to listen and to heed the word of God. Implied in Jesus' challenge is the recognition that if we truly hear his message and recognize his work in us, then we can act on it. In time, there will be Jesus' own stupendous yield in us.

Parables for the Disciples

²¹He said to them, "Is a lamp brought in to be put under the bushel basket, or under the bed, and not on the lampstand? ²²For there is nothing hidden, except to be disclosed; nor is anything secret, except to come to light. ²³Let anyone with ears to hear listen!" ²⁴And he said to them, "Pay attention to what you hear; the measure you give will be the measure you get, and still more will be given you. ²⁵For to those who have, more will be given; and from those who have nothing, even what they have will be taken away." (Mark 4:21–25)

Jesus now turns to the disciples' mission regarding the mystery of the reign of God. To demonstrate this, Mark presents two short parables, the lamp and the measure, along with their interpretations (Mark 4:21–25). The image of the lamp reminds us of the contrast between the secret given to some and the truth hidden from many. Just as the seed is intended to grow, so the lamp is meant to give light.

The lamp, most likely an olive-oil lamp, is not placed under a basket or under a bed, but on a lampstand. Why? Because nothing is hidden or secret (Mark 4:21–22). Those who think that they can preserve or even increase their faith in secrecy will find that they have nothing. Jesus means for parables to enlighten his listeners, which is why he must make their meaning plain for those who have been granted the mystery of the reign of God (see Mark 4:11–12). Part of that mystery is that God will increase the faith of those who give away what they have at the same time he takes away the faith of those who fail to do so.

The parable of the lamp and its interpretation has a brief epilogue, very similar to the one that followed the parable of the sower and the seed: "Let anyone with ears to hear listen!" (Mark 4:23). This time, however, those addressed by Jesus are not the crowd but the disciples, who should not take their hearing for granted—as Jesus has just shown in his interpretation of the sower and the seed (Mark 4:13–20). Not everyone who receives the word receives it the same way and not everyone preserves it.

The theme of hearing also introduces the parable of the measure. These sayings about measures probably referred to the generosity on the part of Jesus' disciples, especially the Marcan church. But the parable moves beyond an economic interpretation.

One who has will be given more; one who has been granted the mystery of God's reign will receive new understanding because of it. One who has not will lose even what little if any understanding he or she has. Those who have not been granted the mystery of God's presence, who are not with the twelve and remain outsiders, will lose even the sight and hearing they had once enjoyed. Everything will become opaque to them. Mark uses the words of Isaiah 6:9–10 to make his point and directs them as a warning to those who receive the word on a path, on rocky ground or among thorns.

Parables of the Reign of God

²⁶He also said, "The kingdom of God is as if someone would scatter seed on the ground, ²⁷and would sleep and rise night and day, and the seed would sprout and grow, he does not know how. ²⁸The earth produces of itself, first the stalk, then the head, then the full grain in the head. ²⁹But when the grain is ripe, at once he goes in with his sickle, because the harvest has come."

³⁰He also said, "With what can we compare the kingdom of God, or what parable will we use for it? ³¹It is like a mustard seed, which, when sown upon the ground, is the smallest of all the seeds on earth; ³²yet when it is sown it grows up and becomes the greatest of all shrubs, and puts forth large branches, so that the birds of the air can make nests in its shade." (Mark 4:26–32)

The discourse concludes with two parables that further develop the image of the seed. The first draws attention to the seed's growth, which goes on mysteriously, inexorably and independently of human effort once it is sown. The growth of God's activity in the world is beyond human understanding. The seed grows and matures all the way to the harvest (Mark 4:26–29). The parable enables Jesus' listeners to see how the kingdom continues to grow without fanfare.

It also evokes Jesus' own life and mission. Jesus has planted the word, which then grows and develops in the course of history. When the world grows to maturity in the activity of God, Jesus will return for the harvest. Mark's audience might associate the harvest images in this parable with the end-time prediction that on the day of judgment God's angels will gather the elect from the ends of the earth (Mark 13:27). Thus the seed growing secretly may be a warning about the suddenness of the coming judgment. No one knows when the hour will come (Mark 13:20–23, 32).

The discourse concludes with the parable of the mustard seed, the tiniest of all seeds—at least in the minds of the writer and the audience of the day. This time the parable does not tell the mystery of growth; rather, it describes the way an extraordinary plant with great branches comes from practically nothing (Mark 4:30–32; Matthew 13:31–32; Luke 13:8–19). So it is with God's reign, which begins as a tiny seed that will eventually grow into God's universal dominion.

Points for Reflection

Mark's parables were a call to action in the particular situation of the evangelist's ministry—a call made to men and women of a particular religious and cultural background and with presuppositions quite different from ours. Already, when retold in Mark's community, they took on a different meaning, for now they were being heard by those who had a commitment to Jesus as Lord and who accepted his authority to speak in God's name.

Retold in our modern world, however, they suffer from the problem of over familiarity. We know them too well to be puzzled by the confused explanation of the different kinds of soil, or to be surprised by the notion of hiding a lamp under a bed. The imagery of the stories belongs to a world very different from our own. Three of the four parables in chapter 4 of Mark are about sowing seeds, something very few of us now do; the fourth is about a wick floating in an olive oil lamp, which is a far cry from an electric light bulb. Those who originally heard Jesus would have been challenged by his message every time they sowed or harvested their crops, or whenever they saw their crops growing in the field and every time they lit a lamp and set it on a lampstand. But we are no longer reminded in this way of Jesus' words.

What then is the message of Jesus' parables, as recorded in the gospel of Mark, for today's listeners?

First, they confront us with the demand to respond and to bear fruit. The reign of God is not about sitting around waiting for God to act, but about doing God's will and acknowledging God's sovereignty over our daily lives. Those who belong to God's realm must accept God's authority and obey. That is why the parables are interspersed with the warnings, "Listen!" and "Those who have ears to hear, let them hear!"

Second, they remind us that God confronts us with his demands in the person of Jesus. If the word spoken *by* Jesus has become for the believing community the word *about* Jesus, it is because the community has recognized in what he said and did the voice and activity of God.

Third, since Christians today may well find themselves wondering, like first-century Jews, whether the activity of God will ever come in its fullness, these parables assure every generation that the harvest is certain, that the hidden will be revealed and that God will ultimately be acknowledged as sovereign. And since the lamp is not totally hidden, but already shedding light, these parables also suggest that for those with eyes to see, the harvest is already being gathered and that the kingdom is already in the hearts and lives of those who respond to God's call.

The contemporary meaning of Mark's parables of the kingdom as internalizing God's activity is encapsulated in a story by John Shea.

The man crept into the back of the church. Early Sunday Mass, 8:00 AM, last row, aisle seat. Barely in, quickly out if need be.

It was his habit since the divorce. He was afraid not to go to Mass and he was afraid to go to Mass. So he snuck in and out. It was not that he was well known in this parish. When people looked at him, they would not be thinking, "Poor Don, what a messy divorce!" But he was thinking it. It was how he saw himself. In his head he was guilty, a major failure at matrimony. And at a young age. It was hard to handle. No matter how much they talked about forgiveness there was very little room for failure in the Catholic church. The last row, aisle seat was a perfect place. It was where he belonged.

The old priest was saying the Mass. He was soft spoken, but if you paid attention, he made you think. He preached on the text where Jesus says the kingdom of God is within you. He was gentle, insistent, quoting from a gospel Don had never heard of. "If the kingdom of God is in the sky, then the birds of the air will precede you into it. If the kingdom of God is in the sea, then the fishes of the sea will enter it before you. But if the kingdom of God is within you. . . ." The homily ended.

As usual, Don did not go to communion.

After communion a woman soloist sang a haunting rendition of "Amazing Grace." Every "wretch that was saved" was moved. Except one. Suddenly the old priest was on his feet and walking toward the congregation.

"I hate that song. I am not a wretch. You are not a wretch. The gospel is right. The kingdom of God is within you. The kingdom of God is within you."

Then the old priest began moving down the center aisle. "This is my recessional song," he shouted

Then he began to point to people in pew after pew. "The kingdom of God is within you. The kingdom of God is within you. And you. And you."

"Oh, no!" thought Don, as the priest approached with his jabbing finger. "Oh, no!"

"And the kingdom of God is within you," said the old priest in a voice that was now quiet, not from exhaustion, but from the intuition that the truth he was saying had nothing to do with loudness.

Last man, last row, aisle seat: "The kingdom of God is within you!"

Don tried but he could not stop the tears. After a while he even stopped trying. Everyone walked by him. Finally, he stood up, walked out and went back home.[4]

For Discussion

1 Who is your sovereign, the one who reigns in your heart and mind?

2. The parable of the sower challenges the reader to bear fruit. Has your faith produced fruit?

3. What do you do with the gift of light God has given you? Do you enlighten others? Do they enlighten you?

4. How is God's presence (reign) in you?

5. Has your faith grown from a tiny seed to a great tree?

Parables in the Gospel of Matthew

"I will open my mouth to speak in parables."

(Matthew 13:35)

The gospel of Matthew was the second one written. It was composed by a Christian community in Antioch of Syria around the mid 80s CE and attributed to Matthew. The language of the gospel is Greek, but it reflects a knowledge of Hebrew and Aramaic as well.

Chapter Four

The core of Matthew's gospel is derived from a collection of Jesus' sayings. According to ancient tradition, this collection of sayings was ascribed to the apostle Matthew. Commonly referred to as the "M" source, it is possible that it could have been written in Aramaic.

The gospels of Matthew and Luke have a source common to both of them, but not found in Mark or John. This source is often called "Q" from the German word for source, *Quelle*. An unknown Greek-speaking Christian scribe in Antioch took the material from "M" and "Q," as well as from the gospel of Mark, and composed the gospel of Matthew from it. Modern biblical scholars follow the ancient custom in referring to this final author as Matthew.

The gospel was not written all at once. The scribe who composed the gospel was perhaps a catechist, who may have prepared certain texts for special occasions. He may have composed the Sermon on the Mount, for instance, to give a comprehensive view of Jesus' new moral principles (Matthew 5—7). Furthermore, he gathered seven parables to express Jesus' view of the kingdom of heaven (Matthew 13). In addition, a string of ten miracles proved Jesus' role as messianic healer (Matthew 8—10).

Such texts were presented to the community, reflected on, discussed and improved upon. Then Christian scribes well versed in the Hebrew Scriptures refined the scriptural references, while Gentile Christians sharpened the universal implications.

In the gospel of Matthew, Jesus tells his followers, "Every scribe who has been trained for the kingdom of heaven is like the master of a household who brings out of his treasure what is new and what is old" (Matthew 13:52). We see this teaching heeded in the construction of the gospel of Matthew. In pastoral instructions and celebrations of the word, text after text was tested, refined and finally approved. Only at the end did the final compiler, technically known as a redactor, sit down and construct the whole gospel, putting various sections into their present places, linking them, integrating, weaving them into a rich tapestry. The name of the final compiler was not recorded, for the gospel reflected not one person's view but the faith of the church.

The gospel's place of composition, Antioch, ranked as the third largest city in the Greco-Roman empire. Antioch also contained a large Jewish population, surpassed in size only by those in Jerusalem and Alexandria. The Jewish historian Flavius Josephus tells us that the Jews in Antioch were well organized. They enjoyed full civil rights. They had their own leaders and magistrates. These Jews had built an elegant synagogue, decorated throughout with votive offerings made of brass. They often sent magnificent gifts to the Temple in Jerusalem.

Life for these Jews revolved around the Torah, the word of God contained in the five books of Moses (Genesis through Deuteronomy), also known as the Pentateuch. All sects within Judaism accepted the Pentateuch. These five books were God's law, revealed by God and conveyed to the people through Moses. They determined worship, ritual practice and everyday morality. Those who listened to a reading from any of these five sacred scrolls knew they were listening to God.

According to a theory among contemporary scripture scholars,[1] the gospel of Matthew was constructed around five collections of the sayings of Jesus, sometimes referred to as discourses:

I. The Sermon on the Mount (Matthew 5—7)

II. The sermon to the apostles (Matthew 10)

III. The sermon on the kingdom (Matthew 13)

IV. The sermon on leadership (Matthew 18)

V. The sermon on the last things (Matthew 22—23)

This construction is not a coincidence. In Matthew's plan for his gospel, Jesus' five sermons replaced the five scrolls of the Pentateuch. By presenting Jesus' teaching in five books, or so the theory goes, the author presents Jesus as the new Moses or, even more, as the new law, Torah, the revelation of God.

The Sermon on the Kingdom

In the third and central discourse of chapter 13, Matthew presents a series of seven parables that concern "the mysteries of the kingdom of heaven."[2] When the disciples ask Jesus why he teaches the crowd using parables, he indicates that it is because of their unreceptive hearts. The disciples (those who have received the kingdom) have, by implication, understood the mysteries of the kingdom more directly. Yet even they are unclear about the meaning of the parables and so ask Jesus to explain the parable of the weeds and the grain (13:36). Nevertheless, they are the ones who have "the knowledge of the mysteries of the kingdom of heaven" to whom more understanding is given and to whom the promise is made that in the future they will have understanding "in abundance" (13:11–12a).

The two audiences in chapter 13 are the crowds and the disciples. Regardless of which audience hears Jesus, they are required not just to hear the parables, but to understand them. Some biblical scholars have suggested that the crowds symbolize potential believers in Matthew's day, while the disciples are those who already are believers.[3]

We will now turn to an analysis of each of the seven Matthean parables of the kingdom as they appear in chapter 13.

The Parable of the Sower and the Seed

[3]And he told them many things in parables, saying: "Listen! A sower went out to sow. [4]And as he sowed, some seeds fell on the path, and the birds came and ate them up. [5]Other seeds fell on rocky ground, where they did not have much soil, and they sprang up quickly, since they had no depth of soil. [6]But when the sun rose, they were scorched; and since they had no

root, they withered away. [7]Other seeds fell among thorns, and the thorns grew up and choked them. [8]Other seeds fell on good soil and brought forth grain, some a hundredfold, some sixty, some thirty. [9]Let anyone with ears listen!"

[10]Then the disciples came and asked him, "Why do you speak to them in parables?" [11]He answered, "To you it has been given to know the secrets of the kingdom of heaven, but to them it has not been given. [12]For to those who have, more will be given and they will have an abundance; but from those who have nothing, even what they have will be taken away. [13]The reason I speak to them in parables is that 'seeing they do not perceive, and hearing they do not listen, nor do they understand.' [14]With them indeed is fulfilled the prophecy of Isaiah that says:

'You will indeed listen, but never understand,
and you will indeed look, but never perceive.
[15]For this people's heart has grown dull,
and their ears are hard of hearing,
and they have shut their eyes;
so that they might not look with their eyes,
and listen with their ears,
and understand with their heart and turn—
and I would heal them.'

[16]But blessed are your eyes, for they see and your ears, for they hear. [17]Truly I tell you, many prophets and righteous people longed to see what you see, but did not see it, and to hear what you hear, but did not hear it.

[18]"Hear then the parable of the sower. [19]When anyone hears the word of the kingdom and does not understand it, the evil one comes and snatches away what is sown in the heart; this is what was sown on the path. [20]As for what was sown on rocky ground, this is the one who hears the word and immediately receives it with joy; [21]yet such a person has no root, but endures only for a while, and when trouble or persecution arises on account of the word, that person immediately falls away. [22]As for what was sown among thorns, this is the one who hears the word, but the cares of the world and the lure of wealth choke the word, and it yields nothing. [23]But as for what was sown on good soil, this is the one who hears the word and understands it, who indeed bears fruit and yields, in one case a hundredfold, in another sixty, and in another thirty." (Matthew 13:3–23)

The story speaks of sowing seed in four different circumstances: 1) along the path, 2) on the rocky ground, 3) among the thorn bushes and 4) on good ground. Each of these is given a corresponding secondary element: 1) birds come and eat the seed, 2) the sun rises and withers the seedlings, 3) thorns choke the seeds and 4) the seed bears fruit in varying amounts.

The concluding words of verse 9, "Let anyone with ears listen!" alert the reader to the fact that the parable points beyond itself to a matter of deep concern. The story has to do with receptivity. It amounts to an appeal to hear positively and to respond appropriately.

Between the parable and its interpretation, verses 10 through 17 deal with the purpose of parables. They refer to positive and negative responses to the message of Jesus, which is the central concern of the parable. Belief and receptivity on the one hand are completely credited to the grace of God. Verse 11, "To you has been given to know the secrets of the kingdom of heaven," indicates that God is the source of the disciples' knowledge as well as their receptivity to that knowledge. Unbelief and non-receptivity, on the other hand, are attributed to the hard-heartedness of those who do not respond.

The interpretation of the parable by Jesus is done in classic rabbinical style, with the disciples being the primary listeners. Thus, Matthew's community could easily have applied the parable to their own failures and successes in preaching the gospel.

In the first instance, where the seed was sown "along the path" (verse 4), the problem is later described in verse 19 as failure to understand. This is not the result of inadequate presentation of the message, but rather of the hard-heartedness of the hearer and his or her refusal to receive. Obviously, those who do not receive the message do not understand it. The birds that eat up the seed can be identified as "the evil one" since, in Jewish literature contemporaneous with the gospel of Matthew, birds are sometimes identified with the devil (*Jubilees* 11:11–12; *Apocalypse of Abraham* 13:3–7). Here reference to the activity of the evil one in no way lessens the culpability of those who reject the message. Rather, it is because they have rejected the message that the evil one is able to snatch away the seed.

In the second instance, the seed fell on rocky ground and immediately produced shoots (verse 5). This is explained in verse 20 as the one who, on hearing the word, receives it immediately and "with joy." At first this response seems to be a success rather than failure. But the story continues with a burning sun that withers the shoots in the shallow soil (verse 6), and the interpretive counterpart in verse 21 speaks of the experience of "trouble or persecution [that] arises on account of the word," that is, of suffering for the message of the kingdom. That the disciples were to expect persecution has already been emphasized in Matthew's gospel (5:11–12; 10:16–25). The follower of Jesus must be prepared for this eventuality and be ready to endure to the end. In the present case, the eagerness of the new disciple is not matched with the endurance under trial. This shows that the initial response of the hearer has no depth; the result is that the seed does not bear fruit that lasts.

The third instance refers to seed that falls among thorn bushes, which eventually choke the seedling (verse 7). Here, too, there's been a hearing and a receiving that produce a measure of growth before the thorns do their destructive work. The interpretation in verse 22 identifies the thorns as "the cares of the world and the lure of wealth." Both anxiety and wealth are subjects dealt with in the Sermon on the Mount (6:19–34; 19:23–24). It is not difficult to see how these things can become obstacles to genuine discipleship and so thwart an appropriate response to the message of the kingdom.

Only in the fourth instance, where the seed falls on good soil, is the seed truly productive (verse 8). In this case, the word is heard and, in direct contradiction to the first instance, the hearer "understands." Furthermore, understanding results in a response of proper conduct. So the good soil represents the one who receives the seed of the word, nurtures that seed in discipleship and bears fruit in spectacularly abundant measure. "Fruit" here is probably to be understood as the pattern of conduct suggested in the Sermon on the Mount: the living out of the kingdom of heaven here and now. Thus, though the parable addresses particularly the problem of unbelief, it also contains a strong element of ethical exhortation.

Points for Reflection

The key issue of the parable is responsiveness or non-responsiveness to God, imaged as the sower, and the message of the kingdom, imaged as the seed. It is in this sense that one either understands (verse 23) or does not understand (verse 19). But there is also the possibility of an initial positive response that proves to be less than adequate. Two instances are given.

In the first instance, we encounter the fair-weather disciple who, under the pressure of adverse circumstances, abandons his or her faith and commitment. This person has thought only of the blessings of the kingdom, having made a simple equation between the enjoyment of them and being a disciple; he or she is unable to cope with the reality of continuing evil in the world. The shallowness of such discipleship underlines the appropriateness of the metaphor of shallow soil.

In the second instance, the response of discipleship is cut short by the ordinary cares of life and the seduction of wealth. The pull of the latter remains a dominant factor in the modern Western world, considering its rampant materialism.

We are, therefore, reminded in this parable of the absolute claim of discipleship. The word of God, when received fully and without reservation, results in an unqualified, constant and abundantly fruitful life of discipleship. The parable contained a challenge to Matthew's church. It also contains an ongoing challenge to Christians and the church today.[4]

The Parable of the Weeds and the Wheat

24He put before them another parable: "The kingdom of heaven may be compared to someone who sowed good seed in his field; 25but while everybody was asleep, an enemy came and sowed weeds among the wheat, and then went away. 26So when the plants came up and bore grain, then the weeds appeared as well. 27And the slaves of the householder came and said to him, 'Master, did you not sow good seed in your field? Where, then, did these weeds come from?' 28He answered, 'An enemy has done this.' The slaves said to him, 'Then do you want us to go and gather them?' 29But he replied, 'No; for in gathering the weeds you would uproot the wheat along with them. 30Let both of them grow together until the harvest; and at harvest time I will tell the reapers, Collect the weeds first and bind them in bundles to be burned, but gather the wheat into my barn.'"

. . . 36Then he left the crowds and went into the house. And his disciples approached him, saying, "Explain to us the parable of the weeds of the field." 37He answered, "The one who sows the good seed is the Son of Man; 38the field is the world, and the good seed are the children of the kingdom; the weeds are the children of the evil one, 39and the enemy who sowed them is the devil; the harvest is the end of the age and the reapers are angels. [40]Just as the weeds are collected and burned up with fire, so will it be at the end of the age. [41]The Son of Man will send his angels, and they will collect out of his kingdom all causes of sin and all evil-doers, [42]and they will throw them into the furnace of fire, where there will be weeping and gnashing of teeth. [43]Then the righteous will shine like the sun in the kingdom of their Father. Let anyone with ears listen!" (Matthew 13:24–30, 36–43)

To begin with, the parable is addressed to the crowds. The surprising element in the parable is that the farmer allows the weeds to grow alongside the wheat. The central thrust of the parable is the contrast between the farmer, who waits for the harvest, and the slaves, who are eager to root out the weeds at first sight. The parable also contains the paradox that the action of the "enemy" (the one who came and sowed the weeds), which was meant to harm the owner of the field, ends up for his benefit, since the weeds can be burned for fuel (13:30).

The immediate and natural reaction of the people to Jesus' announcement of the presence of God's kingdom was to wonder about the continuing presence of evil in the world, particularly as manifested by Roman rule. The remaining parables of Matthew 13 deal with one aspect or another of the paradoxical nature of the presently dawning reign of God.

The man who sowed good seed is identified as "the master of the house," who most likely represents Jesus—a point furthered by the address *kyrie* or "sir," which Matthew's readers would have understood as "lord." When the slaves ask how the weeds appeared, they are told, "An enemy has done this" (verse 28). To the slaves' question about whether they should pull up the weeds, a negative answer is given on the grounds that the grain might be pulled up with the weeds. Both are to be allowed to grow together until harvest time when the two will be separated—the weeds to be burned and the grain to be put into the granary.

The key point here, which will be developed further in the remaining parables of Matthew 13, is that it is not yet the time of the harvest and so not yet the time of separating the grain from the weeds. The judgment motif of this imagery is clear; it is a motif that is found frequently in Jewish literature. It receives considerable elaboration in the interpretation of the parable given in verses 36–43: The kingdom of God has indeed come, but it involves a surprising delay in the coming of the final judgment.

The Parable of the Mustard Seed

[31]He put before them another parable: "The kingdom of heaven is like a mustard seed that someone took and sowed in his field; [32]it is the smallest of all the seeds, but when it has grown it is the greatest of shrubs and becomes a tree, so that the birds of the air come and make nests in its branches." (Matthew 13:31–32)

This third parable of Matthew 13 is filled with catchwords such as "sowing," "seed" and "field," which provide continuity with the first three parables. In this third parable, the kingdom is again portrayed as a present reality. This is the first parable in the discourse of Matthew 13 that does not receive an interpretation. None of the remaining parables, in fact, receives one. So the hearers and readers are left on their own to work out the implied interpretation.

In the ancient world, the mustard seed was known for its small size. From this "smallest" of seeds (it matters not that we know from modern botany of smaller seeds) an amazingly large, bush-like plant emerges, which at maturity measures eight to ten feet in height. It is was large enough to accommodate the nests of birds. This fact was so remarkable that it seems to have taken on a proverbial character. Matthew's final clause, "the birds of the air come and make nests in its branches," agrees nearly verbatim with Daniel 4:21 and Psalm 104:12. These two passages allude to the great tree of Belshazzar's and the cedars of Lebanon, respectively. It is the contrast between the tiny mustard seed and the large size of a mustard plant at maturity that is central to the meaning of the parable of verses 31–32. But Matthew's use of the "tree" to describe the mustard plant probably involves hyperbole, suggesting a symbolism that points beyond agriculture to a greater reality or the kingdom.

Points for Reflection

The point of the parable is simply the miracle of nature symbolized by a mustard seed, which develops from the smallest of beginnings to an astonishing fullness. In the same way, the activity of God has begun inconspicuously. Yet it *has* begun! And in the end, when compared to its size at its beginning, it will have matured into a great tree, where even Gentiles may nest.

It is impossible to rule out an allusion in this parable to growth, even though its main point is about contrast rather than growth. Though the activity of God has humble beginnings, did not overwhelm the world in its coming and can be easily overlooked, it is destined to become an impressive entity. The kingdom's mysterious growth is the work of God. If we view the parable through the analogy of size, then the contrast between Jesus with the twelve at the beginning and the church universal as it is now has remarkably fulfilled the parable.

The Parable of the Yeast

[33]He told them another parable: "The kingdom of heaven is like yeast that a woman took and mixed in with three measures of flour until all of it was leavened." (Matthew 13:33)

The meaning of this parable is that the growth of Matthew's church is as imperceptible as the rising of leaven in bread dough. When a batch of dough is first leavened, it does not look altered. With the passing of time, however, the yeast takes its effect and the dough rises. Similarly, the parable suggests that, while the initial coming of the kingdom of God does not look as though it has had any effect, the effect will become visible and dominant in the course of time—just as surely as yeast has its effect.

There are two added aspects of interpretation here. The woman who mixes in the yeast with the flour is a metaphor for God. A feminine image[5] in a gospel as patriarchal as Matthew's is somewhat shocking. The second aspect of this parable is that leaven is often the symbol of evil in biblical thought (see Exodus 12:15, 19; 1 Corinthians 5:6–8). But Matthew seems to redeem the leaven from this symbolism.

The parable identifies Matthew's church as a mixed batch. This means his church is made up of both Jews and Gentiles. Just as dough is a mixed batch of flour, liquid and yeast, so too is the church, which is made up of males and females of different ethnic origin. There also is a connection with the antecedent parable of the mustard seed that God's reign is as imperceptible as the growth of a tiny seed or the rising of yeast.

The Parables of the Hidden Treasure and the Pearl

[44]"The kingdom of heaven is like treasure hidden in a field, which someone found and hid; then in his joy he goes and sells all that he has and buys that field." (Matthew 13:44)

[45]"Again, the kingdom of heaven is like a merchant in search of fine pearls; [46]on finding one pearl of great value, he went and sold all that he had and bought it." (Matthew 13:45–46)

These two parables appear only in the gospel of Matthew. In addition to the opening formula, "the kingdom of heaven is like," both have the same five elements in the same order: 1) a reference to something very valuable, 2) finding it, 3) going or searching, 4) selling everything and 5) buying it (in the first parable, the field; in the second, the pearl of great value). Although the syntax is not altogether parallel, the content certainly is, which suggests they were remembered together in the oral tradition.

The situation portrayed by Matthew's Jesus in these two parables is readily understandable at first glance. In the first parable, a treasure is hidden for some time and then is discovered. In ancient times, the safest "bank" was a safe hiding place. By burying his treasure, the owner would protect it from being stolen by thieves or forcibly taken by conquering enemies. If the owner died, was murdered or taken into captivity, such treasure would remain hidden, often for centuries, until it was discovered by chance. The point of the storyteller, of course, is that the kingdom of heaven has been hidden by God for a long time and only now, in the time of Jesus, is it found.

In the parable of the great pearl, we have a merchant seeking to buy pearls. The Greek word used for merchant is *emporos* and indicates that the man is not a shopkeeper but a wholesale trader or dealer involved in the purchase of large quantities of pearls. The Greek word for pearls is *margaretes*. In addition to the noun *margaretes* referring to a physical pearl, the rabbis who were Jesus' contemporaries also used the word pearl as a metaphor or symbol for a great biblical text or a sage-like saying. In fact, the synonym in rabbinic teaching for stringing a set of biblical quotations together, such as in a sermon, was making "a string of pearls." So if we take this symbolic meaning of pearls, then the parable might imply that the merchant was seeking a sage-like text about the kingdom of God.

Some biblical scholars emphasize the supposedly different ways in which the treasures were found: by chance (in the case of the hidden treasure) or by deliberate searching (in the case of the great pearl).[6] This may mean that some encounter the reign of God by chance and that others search for it. Regardless of method, both persons are surprised—even for the merchant, who found not just a good pearl but a most precious one. Some early church preachers thought that the merchant's pearl of great price was none other than Jesus himself, the storyteller of God. Others thought it was becoming a disciple of Jesus. So there are many possible interpretations.

Points for Reflection

These two parables elicit a variety of reflections. One is an emphasis on the *value* of the kingdom of God. This is the point of the parable of the great pearl—God's reign is as priceless and as precious as a pearl.

There is also an emphasis on *searching* for the kingdom in these two parables. This emphasis is best found in the parable of the pearl, as opposed to the person who was not in any way searching for the treasure he found. He found it by sheer chance. This may even indicate that discovering God and his reign in our hearts and minds is the result of sheer chance—a great surprise. Another aspect of these parables is the *hiddenness* of the reign of God. This is conveyed primarily by the parable of the hidden treasure. It may be a metaphor for the hidden mystery of the activity of God.

The *joy* of finding the reign of God is certainly a central message of the first parable, for the word *joy* appears in the text. The man who finds the treasure goes in his *joy* and sells everything. The word joy cannot be passed over lightly. Joy is an emotion that cannot be brought on by one's plans, methods or efforts. It is induced from factors outside the self. Unlike happiness that people seek, joy can be present in a person's life even in times of pain (Hebrews 12:2) and in moments when faith is tested severely (James 1:2). The joy of discovering the reign of God is like the joy of finding a hidden treasure. It is due to the grace of God that has shown forth in the person and message of Jesus. When experienced, such joy is the premier emotion of a disciple of Jesus.

Both parables note the *sacrifice* required both to search for and to enter the realm of God. In these parables, at least two common elements make up the "picture" part of the parable. In both a precious object, either the treasure or the pearl, is found; also in both parables the finders sold all they had to obtain this precious object. It seems clear that it is in one of these two common elements that the main point of the parable is to be found. Yet is Matthew's Jesus emphasizing the *value* of the kingdom or the *sacrifice* involved in entering it? Most scholars conclude that it is the sacrifice rather than the value that is being emphasized in the parable. For one, the value of the kingdom of God would be a given for both Jesus and his audience. Surely everyone in Jesus' audience would agree and say, "Blessed is he who shall eat bread in the Kingdom of God!" (Luke 14:15). To emphasize the surpassing worth of the reign of God, therefore, seems unnecessary. Secondly, the end stress of both parables lies with each person selling everything and purchasing the treasure. It is the behavior of both persons in sacrificing everything that receives the primary emphasis in the two parables. They sold all they had to possess the treasure, the reign of God.

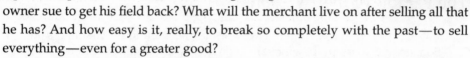

These parables portray the type of opportunity that we modern people might refuse. After all, the purchase of land and a precious pearl involve risk and change. Might not the landowner sue to get his field back? What will the merchant live on after selling all that he has? And how easy is it, really, to break so completely with the past—to sell everything—even for a greater good?

"Seek first the kingdom of God," Jesus says in Matthew 6:33, overriding our puny objections. Greet it with the same spirit as the treasure finder and pearl purchaser. Take the risk! What a daunting challenge for creatures like ourselves who tend to be short-sighted, averse to sacrifice and comfortable in our ruts!

The Parable of the Dragnet

> [47]"Again, the kingdom of heaven is like a net that was thrown into the sea and caught fish of every kind; [48]when it was full, they drew it ashore, sat down, and put the good into baskets but threw out the bad. [49]So it will be at the end of the age. The angels will come out and separate the evil from the righteous [50]and throw them into the furnace of fire, where there will be weeping and gnashing of teeth." (Matthew 13:47–50)

The third and final parable in this section, that of the dragnet (13:47–50), reiterates the motifs from the wheat and weeds. The kingdom is like a large fish net that gathers up both the good and the bad, and after the large catch the good and bad are separated. The eschatological application is that such a separation will take place at the "close of the age" (13:40), when the just will be separated from the evil and, as in 13:42, there will be weeping and gnashing of teeth, a metaphor for alienation from God.

The closing question of chapter 13 of Matthew reads, "Have you understood all of this?" (13:51). The disciples are those who not only *hear* the parables but *understand* them. For Matthew, unbelief is due to the deafness of the hearers, not willed by God. Matthew's message is clear: The failure of the ministry of Jesus, the insignificance of the present church and the presence of evil should *not* be a cause of scandal or discouragement. The ultimate separation of good from evil is reserved for the end time, and the criterion will be whether one is truly just or not. Prior to that time, the community—Matthew's church and the church of today—should be more concerned with their response to Jesus than with separating good from evil.

A Selection of Other Parables in the Gospel of Matthew

While chapter 13 of Matthew centers on the parables dealing with the kingdom, there are other parables in the gospel that merit attention. A selection from the remaining parables in Matthew follows.

The Parable of the Two Sons

> 28"What do you think? A man had two sons; he went to the first and said, 'Son, go and work in the vineyard today.' 29He answered, 'I will not'; but later he changed his mind and went. 30The father went to the second and said the same; and he answered, 'I go, sir'; but he did not go. 31Which of the two did the will of his father?" They said, "The first." Jesus said to them, "Truly I tell you, the tax collectors and the prostitutes are going into the kingdom of God ahead of you. 32For John came to you in the way of righteousness and you did not believe him, but the tax collectors and the prostitutes believed him; and even after you saw it, you did not change your minds and believe him." (Matthew 21:28–32)

This parable appears only in Matthew's gospel. The immediate audience to whom the parable is told is the chief priests and elders (21:23), and it is established in the parable that they refused to accept John the Baptist and his message.

The parable has allegorical features. The father is here, as elsewhere (21:37; 22:2; Luke 11:11; 15:11), a metaphor for God; the vineyard is here, as elsewhere (Isaiah 5:1–7; Matthew 21:33–43), a metaphor for Israel. Each of the sons is a metaphor for the obedient and disobedient within Israel, which will be developed as the parable unfolds.

The first son refuses to work for his father. The refusal is not only an outright rejection of the father's request, but an act of rebellion as well. Later, however, the son changes his mind and goes to work in the vineyard. So the initial refusal is followed by obedience after all. The second son assents to his father's request, but he fails to do what he is asked to do. Nothing is said about him changing his mind; he simply fails to carry out what he is supposed to do. He breaks his promise at a deeper level. The second son even calls his father "lord" (*kyrios*, "sir" in modern versions of the Bible), which the first son does not do. He is all words, not deeds—all talk, not obedience. Clearly the term *kyrios* has a metaphorical significance. There are many who say, "Lord, Lord," but do not do the will of God (7:21).

Now we turn to Jesus' question: "Which of the two did the will of his father?" (21:31). In the response, by saying that "the first" son did the father's will, the chief priests and elders pass judgment on themselves. They correspond to the second son in that they claim to be workers in the vineyard, but they have failed to perform their duties.

In the parable, by way of application, Jesus links his opponents explicitly with the second son. They had given assent to God's law and prophets and were, therefore, like the people who said yes but refused John the Baptist, the greatest of the prophets. On the other hand, the tax collectors and prostitutes made no claims of accepting the law and the prophets, but accepted the teachings of John. Even though the chief priests and elders "saw" the response of the tax collectors and prostitutes to John's preaching, they did not change their minds and believe in him and his message. And those who rejected John rejected Jesus.

Matthew, it is true, is in conflict with fellow Jews, although he does not portray their total rejection. Matthew juxtaposes the rejection of Jesus by Jewish leaders with warnings to his community. The rejection of Jesus by the Jewish leaders of a past generation does *not* determine the decision of subsequent Jewish people. Matthew's work serves to encourage his own community by giving a defense for the death of Jesus, while at the same time reaching out to the Judaism of his own day. The surprise of this parable is that Matthew summons the Jewish leaders of his day to be like the first son and to join the heirs of tax collectors and harlots—the Christian community—while warning his own community not to say "Lord" without doing the will of the Father.

Points for Reflection

The parable asks every reader to reflect on the fact that doing the will of God is more than a matter of words. Words are cheap. Actions cost. The parable also speaks against the view that the ways and will of God are always evident to those who presume to be custodians of the religious tradition, and that they are always obscure to those outside. God may be doing something new—the sending of John the Baptist was an example of this. To reject the new and unfamiliar may not always be right.

What is so intriguing is that God often gets a hearing and a response in the lives of people whom "religious" people despise, like the tax collectors and prostitutes in the parable. These are people who make no claims of being religious, but who carry out daily tasks given to them by God. Precisely when people do not try to be religious, but simply do the will of God through the normal course of their lives, they respond to God's call. That can include both those who hear the parable within the Christian community as well as those who do not. God's activity takes place beyond the bounds of church activity in many corners of the world, even where the gospel has not been proclaimed or heard.

The Parable of the Wicked Tenants

³³"Listen to another parable. There was a landowner who planted a vineyard, put a fence around it, dug a wine press in it, and built a watchtower. Then he leased it to tenants and went to another country. ³⁴When the harvest time had come, he sent his slaves to the tenants to collect his produce. ³⁵But the tenants seized his slaves and beat one, killed another, and stoned another. ³⁶Again he sent other slaves, more than the first; and they treated them in the same way. ³⁷Finally he sent his son to them, saying, 'They will respect my son.' ³⁸But when the tenants saw the son, they said to themselves, 'This is the heir; come, let us kill him and get his inheritance.' ³⁹So they seized him, threw him out of the vineyard, and killed him. ⁴⁰Now when the owner of the vineyard comes, what will he do to those tenants?" ⁴¹They said to him, "He will put those wretches to a miserable death, and lease the vineyard to other tenants who will give him the produce at the harvest time."

⁴²Jesus said to them, "Have you never read in the scriptures:
'The stone that the builders rejected
    has become the cornerstone;
this was the Lord's doing,
    and it is amazing in our eyes'?
⁴³Therefore I tell you, the kingdom of God will be taken away from you and given to a people that produces the fruits of the kingdom. ⁴⁴The one who falls on this stone will be broken to pieces; and it will crush anyone on whom it falls."

⁴⁵When the chief priests and the Pharisees heard his parables, they realized that he was speaking about them. ⁴⁶They wanted to arrest him, but they feared the crowds, because they regarded him as a prophet. (Matthew 21:33–46)

The characters in the parable are the landowner, representing God; the vineyard, a symbol for Israel in the Hebrew Scriptures; the landowner's slaves or servants, representing the prophets who were sent to ancient Israel; and the son of the landowner, representing Jesus. Matthew says that the son (Jesus) is cast out of the vineyard and killed, which is a reference to Jesus' crucifixion outside the city walls. The focus in the parable shifts from Jesus the rejected cornerstone to those who produce fruit.

In Matthew and in other texts of the Christian Scriptures, "fruit" is a metaphor for repentance, conversion and actions that manifest such conversion. "Fruit" in Matthew clearly functions as a metaphor for true conversion. The "fruit" that the landowner (God) sought was conversion in response to the proclamation of John the Baptist and Jesus. For this reason the original tenants of the vineyard are destroyed and the vineyard given to "a nation [people] producing fruits," a synonym for the church!

While admitting that the previous tenants did not bear fruit, Matthew does not dwell on the rejection of the Jews, but uses it as a warning device to his own church community. Writing after the period when the Temple and the city of Jerusalem were destroyed and when his own community was the "nation" (made up of both Gentiles and Jews), Matthew simultaneously warns his community that their status as tenants of God's vineyard should not be a source of presumption. True discipleship consists neither of election nor of proper affirmation about God, nor of mighty works, but having "fruit" when the critical time comes.

The second major emphasis in this parable comes in locating Jesus in a long line of prophets. In Matthew, a prophet is both a spokesperson for God and one who summons people to repentance and conversion. This is true of both John the Baptist and Jesus. With this prophetic dimension, Matthew links closely the careers and fates of John and Jesus and joins their fates to those of the prophets of the Hebrew Scriptures. A defense is thus given for the scandal of the cross in terms of the fate of the prophets, who proclaimed God's will as Jesus did. Just as some of the prophets were killed, so too is Jesus, the prophet par excellence.

In the final verse (21:46), Matthew separates the religious leaders, who want to arrest Jesus, and the people, who hold him to be a prophet. Here he continues the motif that what is important is not whether one belongs to a distinct religious group, but how one responds to Jesus. The rejection of the Jews in the gospel of Matthew is not *total*.

The Parable of the Marriage Feast

[1]Once more Jesus spoke to them in parables, saying: [2]"The kingdom of heaven may be compared to a king who gave a wedding banquet for his son. [3]He sent his slaves to call those who had been invited to the wedding banquet, but they would not come. [4]Again he sent other slaves, saying, 'Tell those who have been invited: Look, I have prepared my dinner, my oxen and my fat calves have been slaughtered, and everything is ready; come to the wedding banquet.' [5]But they made light of it and went away, one to his farm, another to his business, [6]while the rest seized his slaves, mistreated them, and killed them. [7]The king was enraged. He sent his troops, destroyed those murderers, and burned their city. [8]Then he said to his slaves, 'The wedding is ready, but those invited were not worthy. [9]Go therefore into the main streets, and invite everyone you find to the wedding banquet.' [10]Those slaves went out into the streets and gathered all whom they found, both good and bad; so the wedding hall was filled with guests.

[11]"But when the king came in to see the guests, he noticed a man there who was not wearing a wedding robe, [12]and he said to him, 'Friend, how did you get in here without a wedding robe?' And he was speechless. [13]Then the king said to the attendants, 'Bind him hand and foot, and throw him into the outer darkness, where there will be weeping and gnashing of teeth.' [14]For many are called, but few are chosen." (Matthew 22:1–14)

The summary of the parable is as follows: A king prepares a feast to which guests had been invited earlier. When the announcement is given that the feast is about to begin, the guests offer different excuses. The host then substitutes the guests with people chosen at random. Matthew enhances the occasion by calling it a marriage feast for the king's son and describes the elaborate preparations (22:2–4).

Matthew builds his allegorical interpretation into the story, making the parable an allegory of salvation history from the initial sending of God's prophets to Israel through the renewed invitation by Christian prophetic missionaries, concluding with the last judgment when the good and bad are sorted out. The original dinner party has become the messianic banquet—the one that will be celebrated at the end of time given by the king (God) for his son (Jesus), who invites guests (ancient Israel) who agree to come to the wedding celebration, but who then refuse the final invitations delivered by both the first group of slaves (the Hebrew prophets) and the second group (the prophetic Christian missionaries).

The story presupposes the two-stage custom according to which an invitation sent well in advance of the banquet was acknowledged and accepted by those invited, who then received a courtesy reminder on the day of the banquet itself. In Matthew's interpretation, the original invitation corresponds to the call of ancient Israel, who accepted God's covenant. The slaves who are sent correspond to the prophets of Israel. In Matthew, unlike Luke, no excuses are offered. Those who had committed themselves to attend the banquet simply declare their unwillingness to come.

The king is patient and does not retaliate, but sends a second group of slaves instead. This element is unique to Matthew and necessary to fit his version of the parable, for it corresponds to the prophetic Christian missionaries. Not only do those invited continue to refuse, but they abuse and kill the messengers as well. This points to the parable's meaning: Prophetic Christian missionaries are killed, just as the faithful prophets of Israel were.

While dinner waits, the king wages war, kills those who had dishonored and rebelled against him and burns their city, presumably his own. On a historical level, this is not only an overreaction but also hardly possible. The vocabulary reflects Matthew's theology. Matthew is thinking in terms of his new salvation history, not of an actual king who waged war while dinner waited. Most scholars see this as Matthew's retrospective view of the destruction of Jerusalem by the Romans, understood as a judgment on rebellious Israel for having rejected the Messiah.

The first rebellious group has been judged, but the festival house remains empty (22:8–10). A third group of slaves, representing the prophetic Christian missionaries, is then sent with a new invitation. The invitation is no longer restricted to those who had accepted the previous invitation (ancient Israel), but is extended to all. Those who are "gathered in" are both bad and good, corresponding to Matthew's realistic picture of the church as a mixed body of saints and sinners.

How could those unexpectedly herded from the streets into a wedding hall wear the expected clothing, which all but one of them seems to do? In early Christianity, the new identity of conversion was often pictured as donning a new suit of clothes; the language of changing clothes was utilized to express the giving up of the old way of life and putting on the new Christian identity (see Romans 13:12–14; Galatians 3:27; Ephesians 6:11; Colossians 3:12). At the allegorical level, the person who was expected to be properly clothed with the deeds of authentic Christian life corresponds to the "fruits" in the previous parable. Commenting on the meaning of the wedding garment, John R. Donahue states:

The key to the meaning is the reference to the forgotten wedding garment . . . , which is from the same root as the word for putting on clothes. In the Pauline literature the image of "putting on" is used frequently for assuming a definite way of life. Paul tells the Romans to "put on the Lord Jesus" (Romans 13:14) and to the Galatians he writes, "For as many of you as were baptized into Christ have put on Christ . . ." (Galatians 3:27). The community at Colossae is exhorted: "Put on then, as God's chosen ones, holy and beloved, compassion, kindness, lowliness, meekness and patience" (3:12). Therefore the wedding garment stands for Christian life and those qualities which are to characterize those invited to the banquet after others refuse. Those who respond to the invitation, however, must have something to bring to the judgment other than having said, "Yes, Lord." They must be properly clothed with the deeds of Christian discipleship.[7]

The judgment on the person who does not have the proper attire seems harsh; however, Matthew is thinking not of an actual wedding party but the last judgment.

Points for Reflection

The point of the parable of the wedding feast (22:11–14) is that those who find themselves unexpectedly included may not presume on grace, but are warned of the dire consequences of accepting the invitation and doing nothing except showing up. Matthew makes it clear that while unfaithful Israel is condemned, it is not an encouragement to smugness on the part of his Christian readers. The "elect" are not a replacement for Israel, but those finally accepted by God at the last judgment. They will be clothed with the deeds of Christian discipleship.

The Faithful and Wise Servants

[45]"Who then is the faithful and wise slave, whom his master has put in charge of his household, to give the other slaves their allowance of food at the proper time? [46]Blessed is that slave whom his master will find at work when he arrives. [47]Truly I tell you, he will put that one in charge of all his possessions. [48]But if that wicked slave says to himself, 'My master is delayed,' [49]and he begins to beat his fellow slaves, and eats and drinks with drunkards, [50]the master of that slave will come on a day when he does not expect him and at an hour that he does not know. [51]He will cut him in pieces and put him with the hypocrites, where there will be weeping and gnashing of teeth." (Matthew 24:45–51)

The center of this parable is the faithful and wise slave who meets the responsibilities assigned by the absent master without trying to calculate his return. This parable does not indicate that Matthew is developing a doctrine of the "delay of the *parousia*" (the second coming of Jesus); talk of delay is found only in the mouths of irresponsible slaves who think they can predict the time of the *parousia*. There must have been such talk in Matthew's church in the latter part of the first century, but Matthew opposes it. Since Matthew tended to interpret parables allegorically, he probably understood this parable to be directed especially to church leaders who, in light of what they perceived as a delay of the *parousia,* abused their authority for their own self-aggrandizement. Contrary to their calculations, the Lord will return unexpectedly and submit them to a horrible punishment.

Points for Reflection

This passage is about the coming of and the return of Jesus. We might find ourselves asking what we know and what we do not know. It is easy to say what we don't know. We don't know the time—the year, the month, the day or the hour. People who pore over the books of Daniel and Revelation, attempting to crack their code, are fooling themselves. We simply do not know when Jesus will return.

What we do know, however, is what we are supposed to be doing in the meantime. Because we don't know the day or the hour, we are always to be ready. In the context of the gospel of Matthew, that means performing the deeds of mercy, forgiveness and peace that characterize people of the kingdom. Throughout church history, there have always been groups that were convinced that they knew when the world would end. Members of these groups would quit their jobs and wait with eager anticipation for Christ's appearance. In Matthew's understanding of the Christian faith, the second coming doesn't cause us to quit the job of being the church in the world. Rather, it calls us to stay on the job with even more urgency.

The parable is not trying to frighten us into worrying about our fate. Jesus is not seeking to create paranoid disciples, nor is he engaging in scare theology. Rather, the parable urges disciples to be ever vigilant in their expectation of the parousia, the coming of the Son of Man in glory. "Be prepared" is not just a motto of the Boy Scouts; it is the challenge of authentic discipleship.

The Parable of the Ten Bridesmaids

[1]"Then the kingdom of heaven will be like this. Ten bridesmaids took their lamps and went to meet the bridegroom. [2]Five of them were foolish, and five were wise. [3]When the foolish took their lamps, they took no oil with them; [4]but the wise took flasks of oil with their lamps. [5]As the bridegroom was delayed, all of them became drowsy and slept. [6]But at midnight there was a shout, 'Look! Here is the bridegroom! Come out to meet him.' [7]Then all those bridesmaids got up and trimmed their lamps. [8]The foolish said to the wise, 'Give us some of your oil, for our lamps are going out.' [9]But the wise replied, 'No! There will not be enough for you and for us; you had better go to the dealers and buy some for yourselves.' [10]And while they went to buy it, the bridegroom came, and those who were ready went with him into the wedding banquet; and the door was shut. [11]Later the other bridesmaids came also, saying, 'Lord, lord, open to us.' [12]But he replied, 'Truly I tell you, I do not know you.' [13]Keep awake therefore, for you know neither the day nor the hour." (Matthew 25:1–13)

The details in this story seem unrealistic, whatever the wedding customs were. First, the arrival of the bridegroom at midnight seems strange, but corresponds to the image of the thief in Matthew 24:43. Second, the notion that shops where the foolish bridesmaids could go buy oil would be open at midnight also seems unrealistic and contrived. Therefore, it seems likely that the parable is an allegory constructed by Matthew to illustrate and further emphasize the theme of being ready for the coming of the Lord, despite apparent delay.

Vocabulary of the Parable

The *bridegroom* is Jesus at his eschatological advent, his arrival at the end of the world. The *bridesmaids* represent the church, the present mixed group that will be sorted out at the *parousia*. They all have lamps and oil, but only some are really prepared for the eschaton (end time) when it comes. Although the image of God as bridegroom and Israel as bride was prevalent in the Hebrew Scriptures and Jewish tradition and continued in the Christian community, with the bridegroom representing Christ and the church representing the bride, that imagery does not fit Matthew's purposes here. The bride does not appear at all in the story! To represent the church, Matthew needed a group in which the members looked the same from external appearances but who would be separated at the *parousia*. The *wise* and *foolish* terminology corresponds to Matthew 7:24–27, where two men build houses that superficially appear alike but only one of which meets the eschatological test.

The bridegroom's delay does not indicate that Matthew expects a further delay. His parable points out that both those who thought the *parousia* would never take place and those who counted on a long delay, and thus "still had time" to buy oil, were tragically mistaken. Since Matthew designates the story as "like the kingdom of heaven," this shows that the kingdom has a future aspect, that the final coming of the reign of God for which the church prays (6:10) is identical with the parousia of the Son of Man.

The *oil* represents what will count at the *parousia*; it represents deeds of love and mercy in obedience to the great commandment (25:31–46). This makes contact with Jewish traditions that used oil as a symbol for good deeds, while in other Jewish symbolism oil represents the Torah. The problem in the parable was that some of the bridesmaids had no oil, not that they went to sleep; both the wise and the foolish bridesmaids fell asleep. Matthew pictures preparation for the *parousia* as responsible deeds of discipleship, not the constant watching for the end.

The futile attempt to buy oil upon the arrival of the bridegroom shows the futility of trying to prepare when it is too late. Finally, Matthew is not averse to closing on a negative note, with those who say, "Lord, Lord," being excluded if they do not have the corresponding deeds of discipleship. Matthew has already pointed this out in 7:21: "Not everyone who says to me, 'Lord, Lord,' will enter the kingdom of heaven, but only the one who does the will of my Father in heaven."

Points for Reflection

Right at the beginning of the parable of the ten bridesmaids, Jesus tells us that five of them were foolish and five were wise. All ten have come to the wedding; all ten have their lamps aglow with expectation; all ten, presumably, have on their brides-maid gowns. We would never guess from appearances that half are wise and half are foolish. It is not the looks, the lamps or the long dresses that set the wise apart from the foolish—it's the readiness. Five of the bridesmaids are ready for the groom to be delayed, but the other five are not. The wise have enough oil for the wedding to start whenever the groom arrives; the foolish only have enough oil for their own timetable.

Readiness in Matthew is, of course, living the quality of life described in the Sermon on the Mount. Many can do this for a short while, but when the kingdom is delayed, the problems arise. Being a peacemaker for a day is not as demanding as being a peacemaker year after year. Being merciful for an evening can be pleasant; being merciful for a lifetime requires preparedness.

At the beginning of the life of faith, you cannot really tell the followers of Jesus apart. They all have lamps; they are all excited about the wedding; they all know how to cry, "Lord, Lord." It is only as disciples who stay the course that we can begin to distinguish wisdom from foolishness.

The Parable of the Sheep and the Goats

[31]"When the Son of Man comes in his glory, and all the angels with him, then he will sit on the throne of his glory. [32]All the nations will be gathered before him, and he will separate people one from another as a shepherd separates the sheep from the goats, [33]and he will put the sheep at his right hand and the goats at the left. [34]Then the king will say to those at his right hand, 'Come, you that are blessed by my Father, inherit the kingdom prepared for you from the foundation of the world; [35]for I was hungry and you gave me food, I was thirsty and you gave me something to drink, I was a stranger and you welcomed me, [36]I was naked and you gave me clothing, I was sick and you took care of me, I was in prison and you visited me.' [37]Then the righteous will answer him, 'Lord, when was it that we saw you hungry and gave you food or thirsty and gave you something to drink? [38]And when was it that we saw you a stranger and welcomed you, or naked and gave you clothing? [39]And when was it that we saw you sick or in prison and visited you?' [40]And the king will answer them, 'Truly I tell you, just as you did it to one of the least of these who are members of my family, you did it to me.' [41]Then he will say to those at his left hand, 'You that are accursed, depart from me into the eternal fire prepared for the devil and his angels; [42]for I was hungry and you gave me no food, I was thirsty and you gave me nothing to drink, [43]I was a stranger and you did not welcome me, naked and you did not give me clothing, sick and in prison and you did not visit me.' [44]Then they also will answer, 'Lord, when was it that we saw you hungry or thirsty or a stranger or naked or sick or in prison, and did not take care of you?' [45]Then he will answer them, 'Truly

I tell you, just as you did not do it to one of the least of these, you did not do it to me.' ⁴⁶And these will go away into eternal punishment, but the righteous into eternal life." (Matthew 25:31–46)

These are the last words of Jesus' last discourse, a climactic point to which Matthew has carefully built. This is the only scene in the gospels with any details picturing the last judgment. The parable describes the arrival of the Son of Man enthroned in glory. He is king and shepherd of his people; he addresses the just as the blessed of "my Father" and is called *kyrios* (lord) by those he will judge. Matthew thus offers a tableau of titles for Jesus.

A number of important titles used throughout Matthew converge in this scene. Jesus is pictured as the Son of Man (25:31) who has God for his Father (25:34). He is called "king," which connotes Messiah and Son of David in Matthew, and is also called "Lord" (25:37; 44). He is the messianic shepherd who comes for the sheep and the judge who makes the final separation between sheep and goats.

Many treatises have been written about this magnificent story. It is unique to Matthew's gospel and provides a climax to the final discourse of Jesus. Again, the Hebrew Scriptures loom large in the background of this story. Sheep and goats were easily distinguished in biblical times. Sheep were considered noble animals, respected for their silence in the face of danger (Isaiah 53:7). Goats were considered shameful animals, often associated with sin (see Leviticus 16:21–22). Both creatures, of course, provide some necessity of life, such as milk, meat, wool for clothes or goat hair for tents. The Hebrew Scriptures mention these animals most frequently as domesticated creatures, but sometimes they were used symbolically to represent different types of individuals (Ezekiel 34:17–24). Of all the gospels, Matthew uses the imagery of sheep and goats with the greatest frequency (7;15; 9:36; 10:6, 16; 12:11–12; 15:24; 18:12; 26:31), usually in symbolic contexts.

Although the sheep and goats are the most prominent images of Matthew's gospel, this parable includes many others. The comparison is made between the Son of Man who will come in judgment of the nations and the shepherd who separates sheep from goats (verses 31–32). Then the image shifts to a king (verse 34) who questions the righteous and the wicked about their respective deeds (verses 34–45). The questions of the two groups of people (literally, nations) and the responses by the king are highly repetitious, thereby strengthening their instruction. They review what we call the corporal works of mercy: feeding the hungry, giving drink to the thirsty, welcoming strangers, clothing the naked, caring for the sick and visiting the imprisoned.

Note that the king pronounces a judgment on each group *prior* to their request for an explanation about why they are rewarded for their good deeds or punished for their omission of such deeds. In each case, the king explains that whatever they did or did not do to "one of the least of these" (verses 40 and 45) was unwittingly directed toward the king. The sheep (the righteous) are sent to their reward and gathered on the right side, while the goats (the unrighteous) are gathered on the left and condemned to eternal punishment.

Scholars are split on the interpretation of this particular parable, whose language is ambiguous. One group of interpreters maintains that the "least ones" (verses 40 and 45) refers to *anyone* in need and that the nations assembled before the king represent any group of people. This generalizes the parable into the challenge to alleviate suffering of any kind whenever and wherever it is encountered. This view promotes Christian charity outwardly directed. Others hold that the "least ones" in Matthew always refers to the disciples of Jesus. In this case, the parable would be directed to the Gentiles who either treat Jesus' disciples well or ignore or abuse them. This latter interpretation obviously restricts the application of the parable to "insiders" concerned with their own treatment, whereas the former interpretation universalizes the message. Both interpretations are possible.

Points for Reflection

It is important to understand the spiritual teaching of the parable. It draws attention to the practical, ethical application of Jesus' teaching to be loving, merciful and kind to those in need. Such behavior toward others honors God.

We often do not know who the stranger or the fellow disciple we encounter might be. While the scene described in the parable promises a day of reckoning (a final judgment), its purpose is less to threaten than to entice us to live out the commands of Jesus. He is the one who has consistently called his disciples to the greater righteousness and who has challenged his followers in this latter section of the gospel of Matthew to put his teaching into practice and not to be hypocrites, professing one thing but doing another.

There is no escaping the strong ethical vision of the parable. Everyone who would be a disciple of Jesus will be measured against the standards of the ethical treatment of those in need.

For Discussion

1. Do you ever encounter God's activity in your life as a hidden treasure?

2. How does the parable of the two sons (Matthew 21:28–32) cause you to ponder doing the will of God?

3. How does the metaphor of clothing, as narrated in the parable of the marriage feast, relate to keeping your baptismal promises?

4. How is "Be prepared" the motto of a disciple of Jesus?

5. How are the corporal works of mercy related to God's judgment in the parable of the sheep and goats? Is this parable about judgment or behavior?

Luke's Parables of the Kingdom

"What is the kingdom of God like? And to what should I compare it?"

(Luke 13:18)

The gospel of Luke is part of a two-volume set. This gospel and the second volume, the Acts of the Apostles, were composed by the same author and were intended to be read in sequence. The gospel presents the good news of Jesus while the Acts of the Apostles presents the good news of the church and what people did in response to the gospel. In the gospel of Luke, Jesus moves from Galilee to Jerusalem, the center of the Jewish world. In the Acts of the Apostles, the "Way," a synonym for the followers of Jesus, moves from Jerusalem to Rome, the center of the Greco-Roman world.

Chapter Five

Luke's gospel comes from the middle period of gospel writing (83–90 CE); it was written after Mark, on which it depends, and before John. Three major concerns seem to dominate Luke's gospel.

First, Luke may be the first evangelist to understand that the parousia, the return of Christ in glory, might be delayed. To understand this, one needs to realize that Luke thought in historical terms of a remote past, an immediate past and a distant future. For Luke, the remote past was the era of the Law and the Prophets, in which God was preparing a way for redemption. Luke's immediate past was the era of Jesus, the time of the proclamation of the kingdom of God and the center of history, a time when God broke down the exclusivity of Judaism and included Gentiles, women, Samaritans and other alleged "untouchables." It was a time when prophecy was fulfilled (see Luke 4:14–30). The future stretched forward from Pentecost to the parousia and was to be the time of the proclamation of the gospel by the church with Jesus as the paradigm for action.

A second Lucan concern was the destruction of the Temple in Jerusalem. Most scholars believe that the Temple had been destroyed by the time Luke wrote (see Luke 21:20). Some think that, in Luke's view, the destruction of Jerusalem in 70 CE was the consequence of Jesus' passion there. Thus Rome becomes the new center of gravity for Christians. As the political center of the world, it was the ideal place from which to spread the Christian message.

Third, Luke is concerned about the relationship between Christians and the empire. With Jerusalem destroyed and Christians being expelled from the synagogues, the church was in a tenuous position. If Jesus were to return immediately, the church could revile the empire and await its destruction. If the *parousia* were delayed, however, Christians must not only live in the empire, but come to terms with it. In various ways, Luke depicts Roman citizens as sympathetic toward Christianity.

In short, Luke writes with an eye toward influencing Rome positively regarding Christianity. Luke's primary audience consisted of Gentiles, some of whom were Roman citizens. For these people, a literary approach that would not jar educated tastes was required. Using the Septuagint, the Greek translation of the Hebrew Scriptures, as his stylistic model, Luke writes in the mode of a Roman historian, using literary forms and designs drawn from that world. Luke is a classic defender of the faith. To the Romans, who viewed Christianity as having sordid origins (that is, the Jews, who were suspect among the Romans), Luke demonstrates Christianity's universality. The salvation offered by Jesus is available to everyone: "All flesh shall see the salvation of God" (Luke 3:6).

Dedicated to a Gentile, the Theophilus of the gospel's prologue (Luke 1:1–5), the two-volume set commends Christianity to a Gentile world. Luke argues that church and state can live together peaceably. His writings were not only a defense to the empire, but a tool for its evangelization.[1] Furthermore, since *Theophilus* means "one who loves God," some scholars suggest that Luke is writing to all who love God, not just to a particular historical person.

Characteristics and Themes in Luke's Gospel

In Luke's gospel, women have a prominent role, one that at times puts them on a par with men. There are ten named and unnamed women in Luke's gospel. In Jesus' teaching in Luke, women are mentioned 18 times, speak 15 times, and in 10 of these instances their words are given.

In Luke, there are women disciples who provide for Jesus and his disciples out of their financial means (Luke 8:1–3). Two of Jesus' closest friends are Martha and Mary of Bethany (Luke 10:38–42). Furthermore, women follow Jesus to Calvary (23:27–31), are present at the crucifixion (23:49; 23:55–56) and discover the empty tomb after Jesus' resurrection (24:1–12).[2] As the following chart indicates, women are quite present throughout the gospel of Luke.

Women in the Gospel of Luke

I.   **Texts that parallel women and men**

Zechariah and Mary (1:5–20; 1:26–38)

Simeon and Anna (2:25–38)

The cure of a man who was a demoniac (4:33–37) and the cure of Peter's mother-in-law (4:38–41)

The cure of the Centurion's slave (7:1–10) and the cure/raising of the widow of Nain's son (7:11–17)

The male Pharisee who has Jesus eat with him and the woman who washes and anoints Jesus' feet (7:36–50)

II.   **Women Jesus encounters prior to the journey to Jerusalem**

The women who assisted Jesus out of their means (8:1–3)

The women cured: the daughter of Jairus and the hemorrhaging woman (8:40–56)

III. **Women Jesus encounters on the journey to Jerusalem**

Martha and Mary of Bethany (10:38–42)

The woman who declares Mary's womb and breasts to be blessed (11:27–28)

The cure of the crippled woman on the Sabbath (13:10–17)

The parable of the woman, the yeast mixed with flour, and the kingdom (13:20–21)

The parable of the woman and the lost coin (15:8–10)

The parable of the widow and wicked judge (18:1–8)

The poor widow and the treasury (21:1–4)

The women on the way to Calvary (23:27–31)

The women at the crucifixion (23:49, see 23:55–56)

The women at the tomb (24:1–12)

In Luke's gospel, the role of the Holy Spirit is underlined. Often known as the gospel of the Holy Spirit, Luke provides more references to the Holy Spirit than any other of the synoptic gospels (see Luke 1:15, 35, 41, 67; 2:26–27; 3:16; 3:21–22; 4:1–14; 4:18–19; 12:12).[3]

Luke's gospel is also known as the gospel of the poor and the gospel of mercy and forgiveness of God. Luke sees Jesus as friend and advocate of those whom society ignores or turns from in distaste: the poor, handicapped persons, public sinners and all who found themselves related to the fringes of the community. The Lucan Jesus has great compassion for all of these. In Luke's day, however, none were ostracized more than the Samaritans. For nearly one thousand years, these people had been spurned by their Jewish neighbors, who felt that both Samaritan blood and Samaritan religion had been tainted by pagans and their religious practices. Only Luke tells the story of the good Samaritan (Luke 10:30–37) and the story of the cleansing of the ten lepers by Jesus, in which the only leper to return with gratitude to thank Jesus is a Samaritan (Luke 17:11–19).

The most famous of Jesus' parables on forgiveness, the parable of the prodigal son (Luke 15:11–32), is so familiar that many think it was related by all the gospel writers. It is, however, Luke's alone. Possibly the best known of Jesus' parables, it might more aptly be titled the parable of the forgiving father, for in it the mercy and forgiveness of God is graphically portrayed by the father.

Luke's gospel also stresses prayer. Jesus is portrayed in Luke as praying "without ceasing." Jesus prays seven times in the gospel of Luke (3:21; 5:16; 6:12; 9:18; 9:28–29; 11:1; 22:40–46); five of the seven occasions are found only in Luke. In Luke, Jesus prays at every major decision-making moment in his life. Luke provides this as a model for all who would be followers of Jesus.

Luke is also known as the gospel of table fellowship. There are ten meal stories in Luke.[4] When Jesus dines, an outcast or socially unacceptable person is often included in Jesus' table fellowship. Furthermore, the risen Jesus is recognized in Luke in the "breaking of the bread" (24:13–35).

Who Was Luke?

Who was this gifted and highly reflective evangelist? The earliest postbiblical traditions about the writer Luke comes from the Muratorian Canon, which was a list containing the books of the Bible collected in Rome around 170 CE. It records "the third book of the gospel according to Luke, Luke that physician . . . after the ascension of Christ, when Paul had taken him as companion on his journey, composed in his own name on the basis of report."[5] It continues by noting that Luke was a Syrian from Antioch, a doctor by profession and an associate of Paul until the apostle's martyrdom, and that he remained unmarried and died at the age of 84.

That Luke made no claim to eyewitness status regarding the life of Jesus is admitted in the prologue of the gospel (1:2). His polished Greek and use of Greco-Roman literary forms indicate that he had a good education. His avoidance of Semitic words and omission of traditions about Jewish customs and controversies with the Pharisees are indicators that Luke was a Gentile convert from paganism, not a Jewish Christian.[6]

There are three brief references to Luke in the Christian Scriptures. The Letter to Philemon mentions a Luke as Paul's fellow worker (verse 24); and 2 Timothy 4:11 notes that a Luke was Paul's sole companion during his imprisonment. Finally, Colossians 4:10–14 mentions a physician named Luke. Are these references the evangelist? It remains unclear.

The only thing that can be said with certainty is that Luke was a Gentile Christian. He probably wrote after 70 CE but before the end of the first century. No ancient tradition suggests a place of composition for the gospel. Luke's view of Jerusalem, his literary conventions and his vocabulary make it probable that he wrote outside Palestine in a Christian community with strong Gentile and female membership. Furthermore, the special concern for the poor and oppressed in the gospel of Luke suggests that its community had both very wealthy members as well as marginalized and downright poor members. Parables like the rich fool (Luke 12:13–21) and the rich man and Lazarus (Luke 16:19–31), told only by Luke, suggest that Luke's community had rich members who needed to be reminded about their obligation to the poor in their midst. This concern for affluence further suggests and supports an urban origin for the Lucan gospel, possibly Antioch.

Of the synoptic gospels, Luke has the largest number of parables. We now turn to one group of those parables, which deal with the kingdom of God.

Parables of the Kingdom in Luke

The gospel of Luke has three kingdom parables: the parable of the sower (8:4–15), the parable of the mustard seed (13:18–19) and the parable of the leaven (13:20–21). All three contain the same stories found in Mark 4 and/or Matthew 13, all three include the phrase "the kingdom of God" and all three apply the metaphors contained in the stories in a manner relevant for the audience being addressed.

The Parable of the Sower

[4]When a great crowd gathered and people from town after town came to him, he said in a parable: [5]"A sower went out to sow his seed; and as he sowed, some fell on the path and was trampled on, and the birds of the air ate it up. [6]Some fell on the rock; and as it grew up, it withered for lack of moisture. [7]Some fell among thorns, and the thorns grew with it and choked it. [8]Some fell into good soil, and when it grew, it produced a hundredfold." As he said this, he called out, "Let anyone with ears to hear listen!"

[9]Then his disciples asked him what this parable meant. [10]He said, "To you it has been given to know the secrets of the kingdom of God; but to others I speak in parables, so that 'looking they may not perceive, and listening they may not understand.'

[11]"Now the parable is this: The seed is the word of God. [12]The ones on the path are those who have heard; then the devil comes and takes away the word from their hearts, so that they may not believe and be saved. [13] The ones on the rock are those who, when they hear the word, receive it with joy. But these have no root; they believe only for a while and in a time of testing fall away. [14]As for what fell among the thorns, these are the ones who hear; but as they go on their way, they are choked by the cares and riches and pleasures of life, and their fruit does not mature. [15]But as for that in the good soil, these are the ones who, when they hear the word, hold it fast in an honest and good heart, and bear fruit with patient endurance. (Luke 8:4–15)

The parable allows for a variety of interpretations, depending on how one approaches it. It could be viewed as the parable of the sower, the parable of the seed, the parable of the soil or the parable of the harvest.[7]

In the explanation of the parable, Luke talks about the seed first, thus making the seed slightly more prominent than the sower. The seed is equated with the word of God. The parable shows that the seed is fertile, able to bring forth a good yield. Though it appears at first that there will be no harvest, the end result confirms the seed's yield. The parable assures that God's word does accomplish its purpose, even though much of it falls on deaf ears.

In the original context of Jesus' ministry, the parable encourages his disciples that, despite the lack of an overwhelmingly positive response, preaching the word of God does finally achieve God's purpose. Christians today can take the same assurance from the parable. Despite apparent lack of initial results, their efforts at spreading God's word will eventually bring forth fruit.

If one looks at the parable through the character of the sower as representing God, the story centers on how God acts. God is like an apparently foolish farmer who indiscriminately sows seed on every type of soil. The story illustrates God's all-inclusive love. The point is that God knowingly scatters seed on all types of ground, offering the word to all people, regardless of their potential to accept it. Regardless of whether or not all will accept the word and bring it to harvest, it is nevertheless offered to all. If the sower is interpreted to be Jesus, then the point is the same. Jesus preaches the word to all, offering God's love to everyone. Thus, from the standpoint of Luke's community, the parable justifies the inclusion of

Jews and Gentiles among the faithful. The sower has scattered seed among those formerly not regarded as "good soil." For contemporary Christian communities that struggle with inclusivity, the parable can function the same way. Christian denominations and parishes are to include people of all ethnic, economic, social, sexual orientation and gender backgrounds.

The parable can also be looked at from the angle of the harvest. The story cleverly reflects on what the harvest will be like. It sets up different expectations. From the footpath, hopes for the harvest are immediately abandoned, for what is not trampled under foot is immediately devoured by birds. From the rocky ground new hope for a harvest springs up immediately with the newly sprouting seed, which is once again short-lived due to lack of moisture. From the thorn-infested soil, hope endures a bit longer, as seed and thorns thrive side by side. But in the end the thorns triumph. Finally, from the good soil comes grain that has reached full maturity and can be harvested.

The story not only builds up to an expected climax, it assures eventual success in the face of repeated failures. The awesome amount of the harvest breaks open the meaning of the parable. The amounts of the harvest are astronomical—a hundredfold. This symbolizes the overflowing of divine fullness, which surpasses all human measure. It calls to mind Genesis 26:12: "Isaac sowed seed in that land and in the same year reaped a hundredfold. The Lord blessed him."

Considered from this perspective of the harvest, the parable leaves the listener overwhelmed and awestruck at the inconceivable abundance of God's graciousness. It evokes awe, thanksgiving and praise of God, because the miraculous harvest is clearly the work of God, surpassing anything that is possible from human efforts.

Finally, the parable can be looked at through the lens of the soil. This is especially the case in verses 11 through 15, which focus on the four different types of soil, that is, four types of hearers of the word. The various kinds of obstacles a farmer faces from birds, rocks, trampling, thorns and lack of moisture are likened to the stumbling blocks a disciple faces, once having received the word. Deficient understanding, the work of the evil one (verse 12), the inability to provide a place for the seed to take root (verse 13), tribulations and persecution on account of the word, worldly concerns and the love of riches (verse 14) all stand in the way of God's word taking deep root and bearing fruit (verse 15).

From this viewpoint, the parable's emphasis is on the hearer; each is exhorted to root out all impediments and become "good soil." Thus the parable calls those who hear to cultivate themselves for maximum receptivity of God's word in their life. This is to be done with an honest and good heart (verse 15), a metaphor for noble character.

Points for Reflection

The references to the seed along the path being trodden under foot are unique to Luke, as are the "birds of the air." Who is the evangelist talking about? On one occasion in the gospel of Luke the crowd that gathered to hear Jesus was large and became unruly. The people began to trample one another (12:1). The seed was being trampled under foot.

Mention of the "birds of the air" may relate to the story of the prodigal son, where the elder brother charged that the father's younger son had devoured his inheritance with prostitutes (15:30), and Jesus warned his disciples about the scribes who devoured widows' houses (20:47). The word of God can be devoured in many ways. What we do to each other, in word and deed, can determine whether we are able to hear God's word. Our actions can also deprive others of the opportunity to hear.

Although the birds of the air devoured the seed (8:5), they had nests (9:58) and could find shelter in the branches of the mustard tree (13:19). God feeds them. Are we not of more value than they (12:24)?

Looking at Luke's gospel, it is difficult to find examples of "rocky soil hearers." Certainly, Judas Iscariot is one who hears God's word, follows for a while, but in crisis betrays Jesus (22:3, 47–48). The other disciples were also in danger of falling away, but Jesus said to them, "You are those who have stood by me in my trials" (22:28). Growing in discipleship requires that we put down roots that will hold us firm in times of trial or temptation.

The parable mentions three specific "thorns" that may choke the hearer's life: the cares, riches and pleasures of life. The cares of life include anxiety and worry. While Mary chose to listen to Jesus' teachings, her sister Martha was anxious and troubled about many things (10:41). Jesus charged his followers not to be anxious about what they would say when brought to trial on account of their faith (12:11). He also challenged them not to be anxious about what they would eat or wear (12:22). After all, we cannot add an inch to our height or an hour to the span of our lives by worrying (12:25).

One theme that Luke emphasizes is the danger of wealth. Jesus lamented the plight of the rich; they had received their consolation (6:24). Unquestionably, the rich person is a negative example in Jesus' parables (12:16–21; 14:12; 16:1–3; 19; 21:1). The rich young man is the prime example of one whose wealth crowded the word from his life (18:23). Again, Jesus lamented, "How hard it is for those who have wealth to enter the kingdom of God!" (18:24). It is important to realize that Luke's gospel does *not* see wealth as intrinsically evil, but it does see it as a possible thorn that chokes out the word of God. Wealth can get in the way of whole-hearted commitment to God.

The pursuit of pleasure for its own sake can also be a destructive turn. Jesus' teachings often associate the cares of life with foolish living and drunkenness. These can weigh down the heart and prove to be a detriment to prayer (21:34).

In describing the "good soil" the parable says it represents those who hear the word, hold it fast in a good heart and bring forth fruit with patient endurance. Hearing involves listening, but it also means understanding and being willing to obey. Etched on the memory of every devout and observant Jew are the following words: "Hear, O Israel: The Lord is our God, the Lord alone. You shall love the Lord your God with all your heart and with all your soul and with all your might" (Deuteronomy 6:4–5; Luke 10:27). Hearing the word of God and responding in obedience were the very foundation of Israel's covenant with God. Those who are the good soil also hold fast to the word they have heard. They are the ones of whom the beatitude says, "Blessed . . . are those who hear the word of God and obey it" (11:28).

Bearing fruit and enduring are the signs of a mature disciple. This is the person Jesus refers to when he says, "The good person out of the good treasure of the heart produces good" (6:45). Furthermore, Jesus reminds everyone that it is "by your endurance you will gain your souls" (21:19).

The parable of the seed and the soils has become a call to every generation of Christians to hold fast and endure. Hearing requires a strong resolve; endurance requires patience. The word *patience* comes from a Latin verb meaning "to suffer." Often hearing, living and following God's word will include suffering, which, with God's grace, can be endured. In brief, reaching spiritual maturity and bearing fruit requires hard work, faithfulness and disciplined endurance.

The Parable of the Mustard Seed

[18]He said therefore, "What is the kingdom of God like? And to what should I compare it?" [19] It is like a mustard seed that someone took and sowed in the garden; it grew and became a tree and the birds of the air made nests in its branches." (Luke 13:18–19)

The parable appears in all three synoptic gospels and the versions are alike and different in several ways. In Mark 4:30–32, a contrast is made between the smallest of seeds and the greatest of shrubs, which has large branches; birds make nests in its shade. In Luke 13:18–19, a seed grows and becomes a tree; birds make nests in its branches. In Matthew 13:31–32, a contrast is made between the smallest of seeds and the greatest of shrubs, which becomes a tree; birds make nests in its branches.

The parable of the mustard seed is often referred to as a "parable of growth." It is concerned about the growth of the kingdom of God and provides pictorial contrasts between tiny beginnings and grand, magnificent endings. In addition, the coming of birds to make their nests in the shade of a large plant (Mark 4:32) or to make their nests in the branches of a tree is an eschatological image of the incorporation of the Gentiles into the people of God. The same imagery is found in the Hebrew Scriptures (Judges 9:15: Ezekiel 17:23–24; 31:6; Daniel 4:12, 21) and was interpreted in Jewish tradition to signify the coming of the repentant Gentile nations at the end of time to worship the God of Israel.[8]

In Luke, the parable of the mustard seed follows the narration of a miraculous cure of a woman by Jesus on the Sabbath within a synagogue (13:10–17), at the close of which Jesus' opponents have been silenced and the cured woman rejoices. He goes on to speak, apparently both to his opponents as well as to the crowd within the synagogue.

The parable of the mustard seed is introduced by means of a question: "What is the kingdom of God like?" (13:18). In his version, Luke does not explain that the mustard seed is the smallest of all seeds and that the plant is the largest of all plants. The fact that Luke has the seed sown in a garden rather than a field (Matthew 13:24) may indicate that Luke's audience is non-Palestinian and both Hellenistic Gentile and urban. City dwellers cultivate gardens.

The evangelist has placed the parable of the mustard seed after a controversy. The power of the kingdom of God has been manifested in the healing of a crippled woman within a synagogue on the Sabbath (13:10–17). But the opponents of Jesus do not recognize the healing in that way—they criticize him for healing on the Sabbath. Jesus replies that, since one will release an ox or donkey and lead it to water on the Sabbath, how much more should this woman have release from her bondage on the Sabbath? His opponents are thereby put to shame, but the crowd rejoices.

The parable of the mustard seed follows, as though it is an immediate addendum to the miracle and the silencing of the opponents. The kingdom of God, from Luke's perspective, is a present reality in the ministry of Jesus and remains present among believers in the continuation of history (17:21). But its presence and power are both hidden and revealed, which is illustrated by means of the parable of the mustard seed.

The emphasis in the parable is not on a presumed "growth and development" of the kingdom of God. Instead, by means of the great contrast between the tiny mustard seed and the tree or huge shrub it produces, the accent is on the certainty and powerful significance of the coming of the kingdom in due course— God's own time—even though its glory may not be visible in the present.

But the parable does not simply provide information about God, God's kingdom and its coming. In each of its versions in the synoptic gospels, the parable sets forth a message of encouragement. Christians of every age often wonder whether their efforts of work and witness are of any importance in the world. The parable provides hope in every age.

Points for Reflection

The parable speaks a word of promise. The seemingly insignificant acts of work and witness by the disciples of Jesus are of ultimate importance.

It is possible to see big results from tiny beginnings within human history. The story of the church is a prime example, whether one looks at the church as a whole or in its various geographical and ethnic manifestations. But one needs to be aware of triumphalism and of measuring the church's success by secular standards. The church and the kingdom are not identical. The church, however prominent, remains one of many instruments used by God for his reign in people, nature and history.

The Parable of the Leaven

> [20]And again he said, "To what should I compare the kingdom of God? [21]It is like yeast that a woman took and mixed in with three measures of flour until all of it was leavened." (Luke 13:20–21)

This is one of three Lucan parables that feature women as the central character; the other two are the woman searching for a lost coin (15:8–10) and the widow and the judge (18:1–8). The reader is immediately invited to take the perspective of a female character. While the majority of gospel parables center around men, here the reverse is true.

Luke begins this parable with the same rhetorical question as the preceding parable. Both provide an image of the reign of God *(basileia tou theou).*[9] The interpretation of the parable of the yeast hinges on three issues: the connotations of yeast, the verb "hid" (a more accurate translation than the NRSV "mixed") and the meaning of the "three measures" of flour.

Yeast: Yeast is old, fermented dough that is added to a fresh lump of dough in order to start the leavening process. In every other instance in which leaven is mentioned in sacred scripture, it represents evil or corruption. In Exodus 12:15–20, 34, the Passover ritual prescribes that unleavened bread be eaten for seven days. This is to recall the Israelites' hasty departure from Egypt, with no time to wait for dough to be leavened. Eating unleavened bread becomes a sign of membership in God's holy people. According to Leviticus 2:11, grain offerings are to be unleavened, equating *unleavened* with *sacred.* In Mark 8:15 (compare with Matthew 16:6, 11, 12), Jesus cautions his disciples, "Watch out—beware of the yeast of the Pharisees and the yeast of Herod." In Luke's version of this saying (12:1), he defines the leaven of the Pharisees as "hypocrisy." Paul uses leaven as a symbol of corruption twice. He warns the Corinthians, "Do you not know that a little yeast leavens the whole batch of dough? Clean out the old yeast so that you may be a new batch, as you really are unleavened. For our paschal lamb, Christ has been sacrificed" (1 Corinthians 5:6–8). To the Galatians, Paul quotes the proverb "A little yeast leavens the whole batch of dough" (Galatians 5:9), warning them not to be misled by those preaching a different message from his own. Thus yeast was used as a metaphor for uncleanness or a corrupting influence.[10]

In light of these examples, such a singular positive use of leaven in Jesus' parable is an unexpected twist in the story. The point is that like yeast, the kingdom of God is hidden, yet powerful and irrepressible. Its enemies may seek to conceal it, but like yeast it will eventually leaven the whole lump.

It is quite possible that as Luke's predominantly Gentile community retold the story in their day, they may have been thinking of how the Gentile Christians, who began as a hidden minority mixed into the batch of predominantly Jewish Christian communities, were now beginning to permeate the whole. To the Jewish Christians, this "corrupting" influence would have had a disturbing effect on their theology and practice of faith. Having let a few Gentiles mix in, these were now changing the character of the whole community. Yet in the parable this change is in the hands of a woman, who represents God mixing Jew and Gentile, male and female, together into the marvelous dough that will be baked into the loaf of bread known as the people of God.

Hiddenness: The Greek text of Luke says that the woman "hid" rather than "mixed" the yeast into the flour. The verb implies secrecy rather than a normal part of preparing bread for baking. Often this is interpreted to mean that the reign of

God, like leaven, works silently and imperceptibly, surely bringing about transformation from within. This is a valid interpretation, but there may be something more to be discovered in this detail.

Forms of the verb "to hide" *(krypto)* occur other places in the gospel of Luke. In one case, Jesus actually rejoices over God hiding things: "I thank you, Father, Lord of heaven and earth, because you have *hidden* these things from the wise and the intelligent and have revealed them to infants" (10:21). Another text shows that the disciples do not understand what Jesus says to them about his coming passion: "What he said was *hidden* from them" (18:34). As Jesus laments over Jerusalem, he says the following: "If you, even you, had only recognized on this day the things that make for peace! But now they are *hidden* from your eyes" (19:42).

In each of these texts, full understanding of the mystery of the divine reign is concealed—hidden—by God. They provide clues to the meaning of the parable in Luke 13:20–21. In this particular instance, what is hidden is the kingdom itself, and the one who does the concealing is God, who is imaged as a woman. Could Luke be challenging his readers to look for God in the activity of women and men? Could the parable be challenging everyone to look for the hidden presence of God, namely God's reign or realm, dwelling in all who are made to God's image and likeness? Could there be a challenge here to look for the hidden grace of God in the ordinary?

"Three measures": A striking detail in the parable is the gigantic amount of flour being used, three measures (approximately fifty pounds), which is more than enough to make bread for 150 people. Many parables have an incongruous or exaggerated element. Hyperbole is being used on purpose. The large amount of flour accords well with the woman's desire to conceal the leaven. She is preparing bread for a feast or celebration. Interestingly enough, Sarah uses the very same amount of flour when she bakes for Abraham's three visitors (Genesis 18:6). The visitors are from God, and they inform the elderly couple that they will be blessed with a son, Isaac. Gideon uses this same amount of flour in the book of Judges; the text says he used one *ephah*, which is the equivalent of three measures, when preparing for an angel of God (Judges 6:19). Hannah, too, uses an *ephah* of flour when making the offering for the presentation of Samuel in the Temple at Shiloh (1 Samuel 1:24). In each of these instances, the large-scale baking is done in preparation for a theophany, a revelation of God. So, too, the parable of the leaven (Luke 13:20–21) presents the work of a woman as a vehicle for God's self-revelation.

Points for Reflection

The parable of the leaven provides encouragement. Those committed to following Jesus can legitimately wonder whether their efforts of work and witness are of any importance in the world. Signs of success will not come from great success stories, but rather from the mystery of God's grace permeating the life and work of Jesus' disciples.

The parable also reminds us that, unlike human bakers who can kill the yeast, thus ruining the dough and resulting in no bread at all, the yeast that God the divine baker uses can never die. It is eternally living and active.

Sometimes one is tempted to look for signs of the kingdom. As the dough rises, one thinks it is possible to see the effects of the leaven. Surely there must be signs of the kingdom. There may well be, but the parable reminds us that, just like the leaven, the kingdom of God is hidden, and that awe is often the best posture before the wondrous activity of God.

The parable of the leaven also poses challenges about crossing boundaries. It's possible Luke's original community may have understood the parable in terms of their experience of including "corrupt" Gentiles. For believers today, the message may be a challenge to discard attempts at keeping the faith community a flat, "unleavened" mass of homogenous people. The parable suggests enthusiastically embracing the image of God's bread being leavened with persons of diverse backgrounds, who help the whole loaf to rise and become food for the life of the spirit in everyone.

The parable of the woman mixing yeast into dough (13:20–21) is a clear instance in which Jesus invites believers to envision God as a woman.[11] Although God does not have a gender, when we envision a personal God, our human experience of persons being either male or female comes into play. All language about God is metaphorical; no image adequately expresses who God is. God is greater than all the images ever used to describe the divine reality. God is like a woman hiding leaven in bread dough, a woman searching for a lost coin (15:8–10), a shepherd going after a lost sheep (15:3–7), but God is not any of these. Jesus' teaching invites believers to imagine God in such a way that women and men are both seen to reflect God's image equally. When the parable of a man who sowed mustard seed in his garden is paired with that of a woman mixing yeast into bread dough, they show that men and women both act in the divine image to help bring about the reign of God in the world.

For Discussion

1. What have you learned about the gospel of Luke from reading this chapter?

2. How would you describe the kingdom or reign of God?

3. Can the parable of the sower and the seed really appeal to modern people who do not live in an agrarian society?

4. How do you react to Luke imaging God as a woman mixing yeast into dough?

5. Do you think that God's activity is hidden at times? Explain.

Parables about God's Love and Forgiveness

"For the Son of Man came to seek out
and to save the lost."

(Luke 19:10)

One of the purposes of the gospels is to require every generation to reflect on God's love and forgiveness. All four gospels attempt to do this. Luke does this reflection in the form of three powerful parables found in chapter 15. For many, these are the most famous parables of Jesus. As one scholar succinctly put it, "The parables of Luke 15 and 16:1–13 are Luke's *pièce de résistance.*"[1]

Chapter Six

After an introduction that shows Jesus in a controversy with the Pharisees and scribes over table fellowship with "sinners" (15:1–3), Jesus is depicted as responding with a powerful verbal defense in the form of three parables: the lost sheep (15:4–7), the lost coin (15:8–10) and the lost, or more commonly labeled, prodigal son (15:11–32).

There are a number of indications that these three parables of Luke 15:1–32 were intended by Luke to be read as a literary unit. Three features in the parables highlight their essential unity. First, they share a common theme: God's delight in a sinner's repentance (verses 7, 10, 24 and 32). Second, there are certain words and phrases that recur and serve to bind the parables together. Some examples include the concepts of "repentance" (verses 7, 10, 18), "joy"/"make merry" (verses 5–7, 9–10, 23–24 and 32) and "because the lost is found" (verses 6, 9, 24 and 32). Third, the first two parables share a common structure: a man/a woman; one lost sheep/one lost coin; the sheep/coin is sought and found; a summoning of friends and neighbors for celebration.

The structure of the parable of the prodigal son, although longer, more elaborate and complex, is also recognizably similar, with features of loss, recovery, restoration and celebration present. Furthermore, the beginning and end of the material in Luke 15 echo each other, with the elder son's complaint about his father's hospitality to the prodigal (verses 28–30) paralleling the opening complaint of the Pharisees and scribes about the hospitality of Jesus to "sinners" (verses 1–2).

Luke 15 presents an ironic contrast between two paired groups. On the one hand, there are present "all the tax collectors and sinners," who draw near to hear Jesus teaching God's word; on the other hand, the Pharisees and scribes are also present, not to listen to Jesus but to "murmur"—reminiscent of the Israelites in the wilderness as enacted in Exodus chapters 15 through 17.

Their complaint, "This fellow welcomes sinners and eats with them" (15:2), is a repetition of the complaints made by the Pharisees and scribes against Jesus at the outset of his ministry, when he called the tax collector Levi to follow him. And it is a complaint that is voiced against Jesus elsewhere in Luke's gospel (7:39; 19:7). It also reflects the symbolic weight accorded table fellowship in early Judaism and in antiquity in general, where the sharing of a common meal at table was a basic mechanism to initiate or maintain sociability and the bonds of a common identity as well as to distinguish one group or society from another.

For the Pharisees in particular, setting boundaries around the household and the common table were primary ways of setting themselves apart as God's chosen ones, who were called to be holy in a world that was constantly threatened by impurity.[2] One source of impurity was contact with people labeled "sinners"—a label that extended to tax collectors (15:1–2; 5:30; 18:9–14). The specific identity of the people labeled in this way is a matter of debate. As a label, it was a term for outsiders. Used by the Pharisees, it likely connoted people who for one reason or another—occupation, racial identity, physical incapacity or moral weakness—failed to conform to the holiness code derived from the temple cult.

However, the way of Jesus was different. For him, holiness was a matter not so much of separation from "sinners" as a separation from anything that inhibits full commitment to the God who is drawing near (14:25–33). Holiness is not a status to be possessed and hedged around for self-protection, but a relationship with God and fellow humans to be celebrated and shared. After all, Jesus' proclaimed, "I have come not to call the righteous, but sinners to repentance" (5:32).

Why did Jesus give his defense in the form of parables? Jesus spoke in parables because they were a form of discourse that had the ability both to image God in a different way and to open up a wider range of willing responses among listeners than did the discourse of law and purity. Jesus did not respond to his Pharisaic critics on their own terms, perhaps because holiness defined in terms of law and cult restricts the boundaries of God's mercy and love as embodied in Jesus himself. Additionally, extended parables such as those in Luke 15 have the potential, by virtue of their mundane, human, realistic and subtle character, for revealing God in the ordinary. Such parables are an invitation to see God and the world differently, to be converted by a divine grace mediated through everyday stories, whose content (on the surface) is quite mundane. But it is for that very reason, paradoxically, that we are brought closer to God.

The Parable of the Lost Sheep

[1]Now all the tax collectors and sinners were coming near to listen to him. [2]And the Pharisees and the scribes were grumbling and saying, "This fellow welcomes sinners and eats with them."

[3]So he told them this parable: [4]"Which one of you, having a hundred sheep and losing one of them, does not leave the ninety-nine in the wilderness and go after the one that is lost until he finds it? [5]When he has found it, he lays it on his shoulders and rejoices. [6]And when he comes home, he calls together his friends and neighbors, saying to them, 'Rejoice with me, for I have found my sheep that was lost.' [7]Just so, I tell you, there will be more joy in heaven over one sinner who repents than over ninety-nine righteous persons who need no repentance." (Luke 15:1–7)

The parable of the lost sheep contains strong echoes of Ezekiel 34, where God's prophet speaks vehemently against the religious leaders of Israel on account of their failures as "shepherds" of the people to seek out the lost and scattered sheep and feed them. According to Ezekiel, so great is the failure of Israel's religious leaders, symbolized as shepherds, that God himself will take their place in searching for his lost sheep:

[11]For thus says the Lord God: I myself will search for my sheep, and will seek them out. [12]As shepherds seek out their flocks when they are among their scattered sheep, so I will seek out my sheep. I will rescue them from all the places to which they have been scattered . . . . [16]I will seek out the

lost, and I will bring back the strayed, and I will bind up the injured, and I will strengthen the weak, but the fat and the strong I will destroy. I will feed them with justice. (Ezekiel 34:11–16a)

The resonance of this passage in Ezekiel 34 with the parable of Luke 15: 1–7 is strong. Against such a backdrop, the Pharisees and legal experts who murmur against Jesus find that they themselves are under God's indictment for their failure as leaders to seek the lost sheep of Israel. Jesus, on the other hand, acts in accordance with scripture and the will of God. He is the one who seeks out the lost and feeds them.

Taking the parable as it stands in Luke, there are several other observations that may deepen our appreciation for it. First, there is the apparent recklessness of the shepherd, who symbolizes God, in leaving the 99 other sheep "in the wilderness" (thus putting them at risk) to go in search of just one lost sheep (15:4). There is a lack of proportion here that is surprising and almost shocking. But God's activity is like that. God does not fit into our ordinary patterns of accounting. Each sheep is so valuable that the shepherd risks the well-being of the entire flock in order to find it. The concern for the "lost" is emphatic. And that is a feature that highlights a profound point about divine accounting: God counts by ones.

The parable also makes it clear that the shepherd expends great energy to retrieve the lost sheep. Traversing the craggy hillside of Palestine in search of the lost sheep is no easy task, particularly if the sheep has taken refuge in a cave where it might not be plainly visible. And though the sheep may hear the shepherd call out to it, if it has become frightened it will not be able to get up and go to the shepherd. All it may do is bleat until the shepherd finds it. Then, when the shepherd does find the lost sheep, he hoists it up and sets it on his shoulders, hauling it all the way back home. It is no small thing to lug a seventy-pound sheep over rocky, hilly terrain, and yet he does it with great joy!

Then there is the shepherd's perseverance as he searches "until he finds it." Such is the very nature of God! Such is the value of each sheep! There is also the shepherd's demonstration of his care for the sheep: rejoicing, he carries the sheep home on his shoulders (verse 5). What a powerful image for the deity, carrying the lost sinner home. Then, finally, there is the public testimony that the lost sheep has been found, along with an invitation to share in the shepherd's joy (verse 6), presumably by sharing his table. The shepherd, who is God, does not keep his joy to himself. It spills over and becomes an occasion for joyful sociability. The challenge to the reader in every generation is: Will you join in the table fellowship of reconciliation to the lost sinner? Will you dine with the God of mercy and forgiveness?

All of this is delivered in the form of one long question, beginning with "which one of you . . . ?" (verses 3–6). The question is addressed to Jesus' interrogators, the Pharisees and the scribes. They are being challenged to rethink their understanding of divine activity and to respond accordingly. For God's activity cannot be fenced in. It is not limited to "the righteous." On the contrary, through Jesus' open hospitality, God's graciousness is extended first and foremost to "sinners," that is, to those who need it the most.

The purpose of this first parable in Luke 15 is to provide an analogy of the life of God: "Just so, I tell you, there will be more joy in heaven over one sinner who repents than over ninety-nine righteous persons who need no repentance" (verse 7). The emphasis on repentance both here and at the end of the parable of the lost coin (verse 10) is demonstrably Lucan, but it is also traditional. Clearly, the parable is being interpreted by being amplified in a particular direction. After all, neither lost sheep nor a lost coin repents; rather, the lost sheep and coin are metaphors for sinners. If Jesus' table solidarity with sinners is a tangible expression of God's grace and the joy of the kingdom of God, then repentance is the obvious appropriate response—and that goes for the righteous as well as for the sinner.

Jesus compares God to a shepherd and says the same of himself. In the gospel of John, Jesus appears as the good shepherd. The good shepherd, Jesus says, knows each of his sheep and calls each one by its name (John 10:1–30). The parable here in Luke deals essentially with God's feelings: the joy of recovering the lost one. Jesus defines God in terms of this joy. The parable challenges every Christian to embrace such a God.

The challenge of the parable of the lost sheep is whether will we accept the graciousness of God by accepting back into our community the repentant sinner. Every Christian community of every generation will face this challenge.[3]

The Parable of the Lost Coin

[8]"Or what woman having ten silver coins, if she loses one of them, does not light a lamp, sweep the house and search carefully until she finds it? [9]When she has found it, she calls together her friends and neighbors, saying, 'Rejoice with me, for I have found the coin that I had lost.' [10]Just so, I tell you, there is joy in the presence of the angels of God over one sinner who repents." (Luke 15:8–10)

In structure, theme and interrogative mood, the parable of the lost coin fits closely with the parable of the lost sheep. In fact, there is a sense in which the sequence of parables in Luke 15 is really just one, as suggested by the evangelist's introduction statement: "He told them this parable" (15:3). The repetition has an intensifying effect. Like repetition in good liturgy, these three parables seem designed to deepen engagement with the fundamental matters of faith and life. Yet repetition does not mean sameness, for there are subtle but significant differences. Most noticeable is the fact that the first is a story about a man out in the open spaces who pursues his occupation as a shepherd, which is then paired with a story about a woman pursuing her work in the more secluded space of the home. Such a balancing of men and women is characteristic of Luke in his writings.[4] In this particular case, Luke appears to have a special source for this parable, since it is not shared with any other gospel. Taking Luke's gospel as a whole, such a pairing of a man and woman is reminiscent of the balancing of the pairing of the parable of the good Samaritan and the story of Martha and Mary earlier in 10:25–37 and 38–42, or the parable of the widow and the judge and the parable of the Pharisee and the tax collector in 18:1–8 and 9–14. Pairing is found in other parts of Luke's gospel as well. For example, there are the paired prophecies of Simeon and Anna at the beginning of Luke's gospel (2:25–35 and 36–38) and the paired resurrection appearances to women and men at the end (24:1–11 and 12:36–43).

Some may think this is just a compositional technique. In fact, it expresses Luke's conviction that the "good news to the poor" that Jesus announces and what this practice embodies is good news for people of all genders and of all kinds—for "sinners" as well as those who are "righteous," women as well as men, workers in the household, city or country, Gentiles as well as Jews and so forth. To put it another way, God's activity is not a limited good—it is available to all who will receive it.

In the parable of the lost coin, instead of one lost sheep out of 100, it is one lost coin out of 10. This increases further in the parable of the prodigal son, where it is a case of one lost son out of two, with a much greater difference, of course, since it is not an animal or coin that is lost, but a beloved son. So the dramatic intensity increases from one parable to the next. In this second parable, the tension is related to the value of the coin lost, which is probably the equivalent of a full day's wages, the loss of which would cause great hardship. For people living at subsistence level, one *drachma* meant the difference between eating for a day or going hungry.

The actions of the woman, who represents God in the parable, parallel the shepherd's actions, but are appropriate to the domestic setting. There is a threefold movement conveying urgent action: She lights a lamp, sweeps the house and searches diligently. Furthermore, like the shepherd, she searches "until she finds" her coin (verse 8).[5] The coin is valuable, worth searching for, so much so that the joy of finding it has to be shared with her female friends and neighbors. (The Greek is clear here—*tas philas* is feminine.) As with the shepherd, her only reported speech is the all-important invitation: "Rejoice with me, for I have found the coin that I had lost" (verse 9b).

Then follows the authoritative commentary of the Lucan Jesus, which is addressed to the Pharisees and scribes as well as to the reader, that the joy of angels in heaven over the repentance of a "sinner" is like the joy of the woman and her friends over the recovered coin (verse 10). Once more God is found in the ordinary. The parable is an invitation to Jesus' interrogators, the Pharisees and scribes, to be surprised. Living in a patriarchal world, they must have been shocked by Jesus' image of God as a woman.

Points for Reflection

These two parables present images of God that serve both to justify Jesus' inclusive table practices and to pose a challenge to religious leaders. Like God, who shepherds his flock with great care (Psalm 23), religious leaders should go out in search of the lost. Implied is a critique of Pharisees and scribes for not acting thusly. Jesus follows in the steps of the prophet Ezekiel (34:1–16), who had harsh words for the "shepherds" of Israel who cared only for their own comfort. Furthermore, in order to be good shepherds of God's flock, the religious leaders needed first to be able to accept the kind of generous forgiveness that God offers them. But, thinking themselves righteous (15:7), they did not see themselves as needing what God offered them through Jesus, namely repentance, forgiveness and reconciliation.

While the primary recipients of this parable in Jesus' day were the Pharisees, its message is addressed to Christians of every generation. The challenge is to celebrate with God the repentance of a sinner and to welcome him or her back to the community with celebration and rejoicing.

The Parable of the Prodigal Son

[11]Then Jesus said, "There was a man who had two sons. [12]The younger of them said to his father, 'Father, give me the share of the property that will belong to me.' So he divided his property between them. [13]A few days later the younger son gathered all he had and traveled to a distant country, and there he squandered his property in dissolute living. [14]When he had spent everything, a severe famine took place throughout that country, and he began to be in need. [15]So he went and hired himself out to one of the citizens of that country, who sent him to his fields to feed the pigs. [16]He would gladly have filled himself with the pods that the pigs were eating; and no one gave him anything. [17]But when he came to himself he said, 'How many of my father's hired hands have bread enough and to spare, but here I am dying of hunger! [18]I will get up and go to my father, and I will say to him, "Father, I have sinned against heaven and before you; [19]I am no longer worthy to be called your son; treat me like one of your hired hands."' [20]So he set off and went to his father. But while he was still far off, his father saw him and was filled with compassion; he ran and put his arms around him and kissed him. [21]Then the son said to him, "Father, I have sinned against heaven and before you; I am no longer worthy to be called your son.' [22]But the father said to his slaves, 'Quickly, bring out a robe—the best one—and put it on him; put a ring on his finger and sandals on his feet. [23]And get the fatted calf and kill it, and let us eat and celebrate; [24]for this son of mine was dead and is alive again; he was lost and is found!' And they began to celebrate.

[25]"Now his elder son was in the field; and when he came and approached the house, he heard music and dancing. [26]He called one of the slaves and asked what was going on. [27]He replied, 'Your brother has come and your father has killed the fatted calf, because he has got him back safe and sound.' [28]Then he became angry and refused to go in. His father came out and began to plead with him. [29]But he answered his father, 'Listen! For all these years I have been working like a slave for you, and I have never disobeyed your command; yet you have never given me even a young goat so that I might celebrate with my friends. [30]But when this son of yours came back, who has devoured your property with prostitutes, you killed the fatted calf for him!' [31]Then the father said to him, 'Son, you are always

with me, and all that is mine is yours. [32]But we had to celebrate and rejoice, because this brother of yours was dead and has come to life; he was lost and has been found.'" (Luke 15:11–32)

This is one of the best-known and possibly best-loved parables of Jesus.[6] Over the centuries, it has inspired many with its scenario of first-century family conflicts. Its unexpected resolution still offers contemporary Christians patterns of restoring ruptured family and community relationships.

Like all gospel parables, it begins with a familiar situation: conflicting desires between parents and children and jealous rivalry among siblings. What community or church has not experienced some members who faithfully labor for the good of the whole, while others go their merry way, only to end in ruin and in need of rescue? The parable of the prodigal son presents a startling picture of how the path to reconciliation begins.

The story opens with the younger son deciding to leave home and asking his father for his share of the estate. There are a number of unsettling details in this scenario. First, one of the most important values in first-century Palestinian village culture is family solidarity. Loyalty to kin is crucial for survival. Moreover, this was a culture in which individuals understood themselves only in relation to their family, kin, village and religious community. To leave the family was an unconventional break from prevailing social values. Nevertheless, it was not entirely unusual for a son to leave home and try to make his own way in the wider world. One should not imagine, however, that he was off trying to "find himself," as individualistic self-definition was not in the consciousness of this culture.

The second startling detail is that the son demands his inheritance before his father's demise. This kind of request was tantamount to wishing his father dead and would have been heard as a shocking insult during the original telling.

A third detail that calls for attention is that the older son does not object or mediate in any way when the father divides the property between the two sons (verse 12). He, too, seems to go along with the agreement.

The younger son then sets off for a distant land, presumably having converted his inheritance into cash. The parents' worst fears are realized as he squanders all he had on "dissolute living" (verse 13). A severe famine then breaks out, endangering his life (verse 14). Having little recourse, he seeks out a patron, who sends him to his fields to feed pigs (verse 15). To Jewish ears, this adds insult to injury, as the son now debases himself further by living with Gentiles who keep unclean animals. But the son's plight worsens. As his hunger mounts, he would be happy to fill up on the pigs' fodder, but no one offers him even this (verse 16).

Being a resourceful young man, the son devises a plan to save himself (verses 17–19). He remembers how well-paid his father's workers are; they always have more than enough food to eat (verse 17), but there is no need for him to die of hunger. He decides to go home and ask his father to make him one of his hired hands (verse 19). There is no repentance on the part of this young man. His soliloquy, "Father, I have sinned against heaven and before you" (verse 18) is reminiscent of the words of Pharaoh to Moses, "I have sinned against the Lord, your God and against you" (Exodus 10:16). Though Pharaoh's words sound repentant, he was simply at his wit's end with the plagues. In desperation he mouthed admission of sin; in truth, he did not repent. Likewise, the young son in Luke 15:18 is rehearsing a strategy by which he may emerge alive from his dire plight. He knows he has lost his rights as a son, and so devises a way in which he can become his father's hired servant.

The next scene in the parable has an interesting twist that leaves the hearer quite puzzled as to its meaning. It shows the father watching and waiting for his errant son's return and his being filled with compassion at the sight of him. In a first-century Mediterranean family, this is most unexpected behavior on the part of a patriarch who has been so grievously shamed by his son. A more expected reaction would have been for the father to rend his garments and declare the son disowned. Instead he is longing for his return. This is most vividly portrayed in verse 20: "But while he was yet a long way off, his father saw him and was moved with compassion; he ran and put his arms around him and kissed him" (Luke 15:20).

Here we must try to picture the vibrant scene that this sentence draws for us. The son has been gone for some months now. Every night after the evening meal, the old father walks from the house and stands on the mount in front and looks over the land. His eyes travel over the grass, the fields, the flowers, the orchards, the animals, to the winding road. He studies every figure and shadow. He stands there motionless until darkness comes. He strains to get a glimpse of someone. But no one comes. He bows his head and returns quietly to the house.

Finally, one evening the father sees a figure in the distance. He knows who it is immediately! He flings his arms wide open and literally runs over the stony path, cuts through the field, passes the orchard, catches his robe on a branch and pulls it away, ripping it, runs through the hedge and with a last panting dash staggers down the road to embrace the dusty form and kiss the bearded face of his son! Both are in tears. The son tries to say his little rehearsed piece of sorrow, but the father silences him with kisses. They walk exhausted and silent back to the house where, with a new vigor, the father orders a celebration: "My son has returned; he who was dead has been brought back to life!"

What a wonderful, powerful story! Now we must see more deeply into it. We are the prodigal children. *We* have left our Father's house through sin. We have exchanged the virtues and values of home to wallow in the pigsty of selfishness, impurity and dishonesty. We have left our loving God for the attractions of a far-off country. And yet, how does Jesus picture God? As an avenging Jupiter with the thunderbolt of a punishment in his right hand? No! As an angry taskmaster stalking his runaway slave? No! As a cold cynic leaving us to our foolishness? No! Jesus says that God is like a doting father who, while his son was yet a long way off, saw him and ran to embrace him. Jesus says God is like a foolish old man going every night to look for a son who is not there and returning to the house with a heavy heart. Jesus says that God is like that vulnerable father who did not wait for his son to reach him, but at the first vague sign of the son's return ran to embrace him and shower him with kisses. This, Jesus says, is the kind of God we worship. This is the kind of God we believe in.

Thus the focal point of this parable is not the son, but the father. It tells of a father who is a friend, who "first loved us," who out of the fullness of his heart extends forgiveness. The younger son in the story, like all of us, can only wonder. He can only fall down in numb amazement before such tremendous love. He can only acknowledge that it is the father—God—who initiates forgiveness and makes it possible. It is the father who, while his child was yet a long way off, "was moved with compassion and ran."

The parable of the prodigal son provides us with a good summary of what forgiveness is all about. It surely involves the concept of personal friendship and how, through sin, that friendship is wounded or broken. It shows us the boy's conscience being aware, not that he has strictly done something wrong in leaving his father—after all, it was a mutual agreement—but being aware of the demands of love, of how he should have acted toward his father. Notice, too, the boy's repentance, the willingness "to be converted" *(metanoia)*: "Make me as one of your hired hands." Notice, above all, the faith. There was no hesitation or doubt that the father would take him back. Finally, notice the community involvement. The community was called in to rejoice and celebrate. There was to be public happiness that one "dead" was restored to the living community because, since the community was diminished by the sin of one of its members, it too should be present for the enrichment of restoration.

Points for Reflection

The best way to appropriate this parable is to try putting ourselves into the text. We need to identify with the characters in the narrative. The son who rejects his father is me! How, then, do the father's words to him speak to me? The son who stays with the father but is angry with him for forgiving his sibling is me, too! How do the father's words to him speak to me? And the father who is patient with both his wayward sons is also me! Whose weakness am I called to be patient with? With whom am I called to be reconciled? Whom shouldd I forgive?

Interestingly enough, the story ends with a play on words: "This son of mine was dead and is alive again; he was lost and is found!" When the father leaves the older son in the field, these are his last words to him: "This brother of yours was dead and has come to life; he was lost and has been found." If the reader/listener of the parable continues with the unspoken analogy, this could be its message: "Now you are dead and lost, unless you come in."

The parable concludes there, with the father going back into the house to the celebration, leaving the elder brother to decide. The invitation to intimacy remains; the challenge is to respond, for the story invites us to come in and celebrate someone else's acceptance of God's mercy and forgiveness. Then perhaps we will be able to accept the mercy, too.

The parable of the prodigal son, like all good stories, is about us. It is told by Jesus and, as the great rabbi Baal Shem Tov, the founder of Hasidic Judaism, would say: "When someone comes to you and tells you your own story, you know that your sins are forgiven. And when you are forgiven, you are healed."

For Discussion

1. How do the parables presented in this chapter relate to your images for God? Explain.

2. Are there times in your life when you feel you have been lost and then found by God?

3. How precious are you in God's eyes?

4. Have you ever felt or experienced the forgiveness of God? Describe that feeling or experience.

5. Try this exercise. Read the parable of the prodigal son three times. In the first reading, identify yourself with the younger son. In the second reading with the father. In the third with the older son. What happened to you as a result of doing this exercise? Explain.

Parables about Poverty and Riches

"For you always have the poor with you, and you can show kindness to them whenever you wish."

(Mark 14:7)

J esus' parables of the rich fool (Luke 12:13–21), the shrewd manager (Luke 16:1–13) and the rich man and Lazarus (Luke 16:19–31) have as their central theme issues concerning poverty and riches. They warn against the allure of wealth, not because wealth is intrinsically evil, but because it can get in the way of a person's wholehearted commitment to God. In addition, these parables provide for the poor a way of liberation by forsaking the illusion of materialsim for trust in the God of justice.[1] Simultaneously, these parables summon the rich to repentance; they hold in healthy tension the prophetic and the practical.

Chapter Seven

Each of these parables begins with the phrase "a rich man," which invites the modern reader to locate these words in both their first-century context as well as the current world. Furthermore, these words indicate of how a character emerges in a story. The way a storyteller gives character to a figure in a story and the way an audience understands that characterization depend on a general understanding of the figure's role in the society of the day.

Along with other ancient agrarian societies, Israel was marked by stark disparity between a small, wealthy ruling class and a large number of peasants who barely eked out a living from their tiny plots of land. The rich maintained and enhanced their status and wealth by extracting labor and tribute from the poor.

These three Lucan parables are set in contexts that imply they were addressed to both private and public audiences. These audiences were composed of the rich and the poor, the crowds, the disciples and the Pharisees. The parable of the rich fool (12:13–21) is directed to a crowd of people who had gathered around Jesus; the parable of the shrewd manager (16:1–13) is addressed by Jesus explicitly to "his disciples" (verse 1); and the parable of the rich man and Lazarus (16:19–31) is addressed to the Pharisees. Luke has connected the three parables literarily to highlight their application to different groups of people, with these diverse groups serving to represent the whole of society in Jesus' day. Jesus warns the crowds—and particularly his disciples—not to fear their poverty or to imitate those who aspire to be rich. It is important to realize that such a warning in and of itself does not imply a blanket rejection of the rich; Jesus appeals to them as well as to the poor. These parables require readers of every generation to reflect seriously on poverty and wealth in relation to the practice of faith.

Parable of the Rich Fool

13Someone in the crowd said to him, "Teacher, tell my brother to divide the family inheritance with me." 14But he said to him, "Friend, who set me to be a judge or arbitrator over you?" 15And he said to them, "Take care! Be on your guard against all kinds of greed; for one's life does not consist in the abundance of possessions." 16Then he told them a parable: "The land of a rich man produced abundantly. 17And he thought to himself, 'What should I do, for I have no place to store my crops?' 18Then he said, 'I will do this: I will pull down my barns and build larger ones, and there I will store all my grain and my goods. 19And I will say to my soul, 'Soul, you have ample goods laid up for many years; relax, eat, drink, be merry.' 20But God said to him, 'You fool! This very night your life is being demanded of you. And the things you have prepared, whose will they be?' 21So it is with those who store up treasures for themselves but are not rich toward God." (Luke 12:13–21)

This parable is presented as part of Jesus' answer to a man calling on him to settle an inheritance dispute between himself and his brother (verse 13). Jesus proposes no instant solution. Rather, he points out to both parties the heart of the problem—greed or covetousness. While Jesus' warning against covetousness is shocking, it is also realistic and practical. If both disputants would abandon greed, a way forward could be discerned.

A reason is added to the warning: "One's life does not consist in the abundance of possessions" (12:15). "Abundance" suggests the surpluses that sustained the wealth and status of the elite members of society. Though frequently taken as pitting material life against spiritual life, it is probably better to read this saying as contrasting luxury with necessity. Thus peasants are not to be deluded by the harshness of their poverty into thinking that life means having more than one needs. In other words, do not be deceived into thinking that the solution to poverty is to be found in imitating the delight of the elite in their excesses. Opulence is not the other side of the coin of poverty—justice is.

In Jesus' telling of the story, his hearers are given a glimpse into the rich man's thinking, which would have been readily recognizable to them in that day. The man's plans were in line with ancient suggestions that farmers make the greatest use possible of their productive land. So the rich man decided not to add new barns to his alreaady existing ones, but to tear down his old barns and build more spacious and efficient ones on the same site (verses 17–18). Grain could be kept for a number of years. Perhaps he thought that he would get a better price for it at some later time. Regardless, he foresaw that this great surplus could finance a life of comfort, luxury and ease (verse 19). The saying "relax, eat, drink, be merry" (12:19) represents the typical outlook of a hedonist.

God dramatically interrupts the rich man's thought processes. Interestingly enough, no other parable has a direct appearance by God.[2] God calls him "a fool," that is, one who "has said in his heart: 'There is no God'" (Psalm 14). He is a fool because his own life is about to be "demanded" of him, and all his goods will then pass into other hands. The illusion of ownership he has maintained will be shattered. The things he has regarded as his will be his no more. Even his soul, or life, which he had called "mine" and planned to pamper indefinitely, is the very same soul or life that is suddenly revealed as a loan, not a possession, and is now required of him (verse 20).

The closing comment of the parable in verse 21, "So it is with those who store up treasure for themselves but are not rich toward God," crystallizes its message by pointing to the contrast between "storing up treasures" for oneself, as this man did, and being "rich toward God." The verses that follow the parable, which urge trust in God and almsgiving, describe what it means to be "rich toward God" (12:22–34).

We miss the force of the story if we see the rich man as being especially wicked. His thought processes are normal. They form the whole basis of an exploitive, agrarian society that seeks control over land and wants to use surpluses to finance luxury. These are thought processes that exclude God and other people—who both inevitably reassert themselves at the end.

The flaw that besets the rich fool was that he was consumed with his possessions and that the meaning and value of his life depended on them. The man and his possessions are so intimately tied together that they are inseparable. In the

English translation of the parable, the personal pronoun "I" shows up six times and the possessive "my" five times ("my crops," "my barns," "my grain," "my goods," and "my soul" [NRSV]).

The parable provides an example of what one ought not to be like. The person whose identity is tied up with his or her possessions, status and achievements, and who is driven by acquiring them, can easily end up unaware of the call of God and the need of the neighbor. The alternative is a life that is "rich toward God," one that is devoted to serving God on a daily basis, which includes having eyes open to the needs of others. "Riches can cause blindness to God and to the presence of the neighbor; they can isolate people from community; the Christian community must embody the good news of the poor; material possessions, which are a gift from God, are to be used in service of the poor."[3]

Points for Reflection

The parable never states exactly what the rich man's folly was. This allows the parable to be reflected on from a variety of angles.

Possessions: The fool's goods and prosperity have become the sole pursuit of his life, until finally the poverty of his abundance is exposed. The parable requires the hearer of every generation to reflect on the relationship of possessions to the meaning of life. The adage, "Whoever dies with the most toys wins," is exploded by the parable, which exposes the emptiness of such a materialistic lifestyle.

Self-sufficiency: The parable sketches the figure of a person who does not need anyone else. He or she does not feel the need of a community or God's love. The parable thus allows the reader to reflect on the pride-filled inclination to think that we can make it on our own and that we don't need anyone else. The parable smashes the unhealthy American myth of "being able to pull ourselves up by our own bootstraps."

Greed: Greed is the opposite of generosity. The thought of what he might have been able to do for those in need never entered the rich fool's mind. Greed has eaten away any compassion he may have had. The parable forces the reader to come to grips with greed in his or her own life.

Hedonism: The rich fool revels in his prosperity because he envisions that, due to his wealth, he can "eat, drink and be merry." The greatest good he can imagine is a life of maximizing his own pleasure. The parable plunges the reader into reflecting on his or her own temptation to hedonism. This is a virulent temptation at the dawn of the twenty-first century, where technology and consumerism, the current brand of hedonism, thrive in first-world countries.

Atheism: The rich fool may claim he has always believed in God, but when it comes to managing his own life, dealing with possessions and planning for the future, he lives as though there were no God. It would be fair to call him a functional atheist. The parable therefore confronts our basic commitments. What difference does or should our faith in God make in the practical matters of life?

The Parable of the Shrewd Manager

¹Then Jesus said to the disciples, "There was a rich man who had a manager, and charges were brought to him that this man was squandering his property. ²So he summoned him and said to him, 'What is this that I hear about you? Give me an accounting of your management, because you cannot be my manager any longer.' ³Then the manager said to himself, 'What will I do, now that my master is taking the position away from me? I am not strong enough to dig, and I am ashamed to beg. ⁴I have decided what to do so that, when I am dismissed as manager, people may welcome me into their homes.' ⁵So, summoning his master's debtors one by one, he asked the first, 'How much do you owe my master?' ⁶He answered, 'A hundred jugs of olive oil.' He said to him, 'Take your bill, sit down quickly and make it fifty.' ⁷Then he asked another, 'And how much do you owe?' He replied, 'A hundred containers of wheat.' He said to him, 'Take your bill and make it eighty.' ⁸And his master commended the dishonest manager because he had acted shrewdly; for the children of this age are more shrewd in dealing with their own generation than are the children of light. ⁹And I tell you, make friends for yourselves by means of dishonest wealth so that when it is gone, they may welcome you into the eternal homes.

¹⁰"Whoever is faithful in a very little is faithful also in much; and whoever is dishonest in a very little is dishonest also in much. ¹¹If then you have not been faithful with the dishonest wealth, who will entrust to you the true riches? ¹²And if you have not been faithful with what belongs to another, who will give you what is your own? ¹³No slave can serve two masters; for a slave will either hate the one and love the other, or be devoted to the one and despise the other. You cannot serve God and wealth." (Luke 16:1–13)

The parable is addressed to Jesus' disciples. The story concerns two figures: a rich man and the manager of his wealth. The rich man may have been an absentee landowner who had a manager for his property. The story begins when charges are brought to the rich man that the manager has been "squandering his property." These charges echo the actions of the prodigal son (15:13). Just as the parable of the rich fool and the parable of the prodigal son feature interior monologues, so too does the manager's interior speech, which is a significant turning point in the parable. Like the rich fool (12:17), he asks himself, "What will I do?" He is addressing the rich man as "my master"—a better translation would be "My lord" (*kyrios*)—in verse 3 and prepares for its occurrence in verse 8. In distress, the manager considers his  options. To dig? "I am not strong enough." To beg? "I am too ashamed." Instead his interior monologue tells us that he has seized on an alternative that will make him welcome in others' homes after he has been dismissed by his master. This course of action is not explained, however, so the reader's suspense and curiosity build while the manager proceeds with his plans.

In response to the imminent crisis, the manager calls in the master's debtors and summarily reduces the debt of each. In the situation presumed by the story, the master has apparently rented his land to tenants who have agreed to pay him a fixed return in grain or oil. The size of the reduction seems to reflect the arbitrariness of the manager's actions. A debt of 100 jugs of olive oil is reduced to 50; a debt of 100 containers of wheat is reduced to 80.

By reducing the amount of the debts while he is still in the service of the rich man, or at least while the debtors still assume that he is the rich man's manager, he will gain their favor. The rich man will not be able to reverse his actions later without losing face with his debtors, and the manager will have acquired a debt of honor and gratitude from each debtor that will ensure their goodwill toward him in the future. The chief difficulty in interpreting the parable concerns the manager's action in reducing the debts. Was he dishonestly falsifying the records in order to gain the favor of the debtors, or was he shrewdly sacrificing his own prospect of short-term gain for long-term benefits? It is very hard to know the answer to this question.

The greatest challenge voiced in the parable is in verse 10: "Whoever is faithful in a very little is faithful also in much; and whoever is dishonest in a very little is dishonest also in much." Faithfulness and honesty are not related to wealth and power. One who is faithful over a little amount will be faithful over a large one. The contrast between little and much is then applied in two ways. First, in verse 11, if one has not been faithful over worldly wealth, how can that person be trusted with true wealth? Second, in verse 12, if you have not been faithful over what belongs to another—the worldly wealth God has entrusted to you—then who will give you your own treasure in heaven?

The parable emphasizes that the chief responsibility of a disciple of Jesus is to be faithful even in small things. One interpreter vividly and insightfully grasps the force of the saying in verse 10:

> Most of us will not this week christen a ship, write a book, end a war, appoint a cabinet, dine with a queen, convert a nation, or be burned at the stake. More likely the week will present no more than a chance to give a cup of water, write a note, visit a nursing home, vote for a county commissioner, teach a Sunday school class, share a meal, tell a child a story, go to choir practice and feed the neighbor's cat. "Whoever is faithful in very little is faithful also in much."[4]

The Parable of the Rich Man and Lazarus

[19]"There was a rich man who was dressed in purple and fine linen and who feasted sumptuously every day. [20]And at his gate lay a poor man named Lazarus, covered with sores, [21]who longed to satisfy his hunger with what fell from the rich man's table; even the dogs would come and

lick his sores. ²²The poor man died and was carried away by the angels to be with Abraham. The rich man also died and was buried. ²³In Hades, where he was being tormented, he looked up and saw Abraham far away with Lazarus by his side. ²⁴He called out, 'Father Abraham, have mercy on me, and send Lazarus to dip the tip of his finger in water and cool my tongue; for I am in agony in these flames.' ²⁵But Abraham said, 'Child, remember that during your lifetime you received your good things, and Lazarus in like manner evil things; but now he is comforted here, and you are in agony. ²⁶Besides all this, between you and us a great chasm has been fixed, so that those who might want to pass from here to you cannot do so, and no one can cross from there to us.' ²⁷He said, 'Then, father, I beg you to send him to my father's house—²⁸for I have five brothers—that he may warn them, so that they will not also come into this place of torment.' ²⁹Abraham replied, 'They have Moses and the prophets; they should listen to them.' ³⁰He said, 'No, father Abraham; but if someone goes to them from the dead, they will repent.' ³¹He said to him, 'If they do not listen to Moses and the prophets, neither will they be convinced even if someone rises from the dead.'" (Luke 16:19–31)

This parable can be viewed as a drama in three acts. In the first act, the rich appear to be rich and the poor to be poor. The first act, however, is a tableau. The characters are introduced and their way of life is described, but nothing happens. There is no interaction between the rich man and Lazarus. The measure of the man's wealth is illustrated by his conspicuous consumption—his dress and his diet. The rich man wears purple, which may mean that he was a high-ranking official or member of the royal family. The Romans had set standards regarding who could wear purple and how much purple they could wear. The rich man lived in a house with gates for privacy or security—for separation from the riff-raff of the city. He dressed in fine linen and feasted sumptuously every day. He had everything a person could want. The story will quickly make clear, however, that the glitter of the rich man's life was superficial and transient. It had nothing to do with the eternal glory that surrounds the Lord.

The next verses (20–21) introduce Lazarus, the only character in any of Jesus' parables who is given a name. The name is part of the characterization, because it comes from Eleazar, which means "God helps," and thus foreshadows Lazarus' fate. Tragically, no one else helps Lazarus. He is a beggar, lying before the rich man's gate, and his body is covered with running sores. He would gladly have been "filled" with the soiled bread from the rich man's table. At a feast, bread was used to wipe the grease from one's hands and then thrown under the table. The depth of Lazarus' deprivation is described with one final detail: the dogs (which probably ate scraps from the rich man's table) licked his sores as they passed by. Lazarus dies of starvation and disease at the rich man's gate. The first act ends after we have met the two characters. Neither character speaks to the other; their lives seem to be entirely separate, divided by a table and a gate.

In the second act, which begins in verse 22 of chapter 16, the rich become poor and the poor become rich. The rich man was introduced first, as one would expect, and then Lazarus. Now Lazarus' death, which comes as no surprise, is reported first, then the death of the rich man. Lazarus' death underscores the urgency of Jesus' challenge to the well-to-do: When you give a feast, do not invite your friends and rich neighbors. Instead, invite "the poor, the crippled, the lame and the blind" (Luke 14:13).

The parable does not dwell on Lazarus' death. At his death, he is transported by angels to the bosom of Abraham, which is a metaphor for being in a high spot, close to God in heaven. Nothing is said of Lazarus' burial.[5] Again, our imaginations attempt to fill the gap in the story. Neglected by others, Lazarus is prized in the sight of God. Unexpectedly, we are told that the rich man has died also. The contrast between the two characters is again drawn with verb usage. While Lazarus is "carried away by angels," the rich man is simply "buried," probably in the purple robes in which he had lived.

The third act (verses 23–31) is by far the longest and most developed. For the first time, narration gives way to dialogue, with three complete exchanges between the rich man and Abraham. The third act is the climax of the story, the focal point of the parable. In the third act, the poor are rich and the rich are poor.

The "bosom of Abraham" was regarded as the place of highest bliss according to Jewish tradition. Being in the bosom of Abraham may imply that Lazarus was the honored guest at the heavenly banquet, feasting while the rich man was in torment. How ironically the table has turned.

To many who heard the parable, this turn of events would have come as a surprise, for it was believed at the time of Jesus that blessings and wealth in this life were a sign of God's favor, while illness, poverty and hardship were signs of God's displeasure. A just God would not do otherwise. How could a beggar go to heaven? Easily, Jesus says, for admission to the presence of God is not determined by wealth, but by faith in God and concern for the marginalized.

There are three exchanges between the rich man and Abraham. Lazarus, who never asked for anything on earth, never says anything in heaven. Abraham now speaks for the beggar who has no voice. In the first exchange, the rich man asks "Father Abraham" to send Lazarus to dip his finger in water to cool his tongue. The text is typical hyperbole. By addressing Abraham as "Father," he may imply that he too should be recognized as a "son of Abraham." Because he knows Lazarus' name, we may assume that the rich man had known Lazarus' plight and had done nothing. But is that worse than if he had not even known of the suffering of the beggar at his gate? Either way, the rich man still regards Lazarus as being available to serve his personal needs: "Send Lazarus."

Abraham responds, acknowledging the rich man with the address, "child." Being a child of Abraham, therefore, is no guarantee that one will dwell with Abraham in paradise. The reversal sequence of Abraham's response again serves to connect the lives and rewards of the rich man and Lazarus: "Remember that during your lifetime you received good things and Lazarus in like manner evil things; but now he is comforted here and you are in agony" (verse 25). Remembering can either be part of one's torment, as here, or part of one's salvation. In life, the beggar got only discarded goods and was treated shamefully. Now the men's fates are reversed.

The chasm that now separates the rich man and Lazarus confirms the finality of the judgment on the rich man. Once there was no chasm but indifference and apathy. The rich man could have come to Lazarus at any time. Now, however, the chasm that separates them prevents Lazarus from responding to the rich man's torment with compassion and removes any possibility that the rich man might escape his torment. The rich man has shut himself off from Lazarus, and now no one can reach him.

In the second exchange (16:27–28), the rich man asks Abraham to send Lazarus to warn the rich man's five brothers. If there is no hope for him, at least he may be able to intervene and spare his brothers. The reference to his extended family as "my father's house" contrasts with his earlier use of "Father Abraham." Admirably, he thinks of someone other than himself for the first time in the story, but he still assumes that Lazarus can be his errand boy.

Abraham's response to the rich man's second request is that the brothers have Moses and the prophets. Did Moses not say, "Do not be hardhearted or tight-fisted toward your needy neighbor" (Deuteronomy 15:7)? And are not the words of Isaiah clear enough?

> [6]Is not this the fast that I choose: to loose the bonds of injustice, to undo the thongs of the yoke, to let the oppressed go free, and to break every yoke? [7]Is it not to share your bread with the hungry, and bring the homeless poor into your house; when you see the naked, to cover them, and not to hide yourself from your own kin? (Isaiah 58:6–7)

Abraham's response, which concludes the parable, adds finality to the urgency of hearing Moses and the prophets. If the brothers will not hear them, then they will not be convinced, even if one should rise from the dead. The language echoes the proclamation of Jesus' resurrection. Until this point, resurrection has not been mentioned. The rich man's request may be understood as an appeal for Lazarus to warn to his brothers in a dream or a vision. Abraham's response, however, foreshadows the resurrection of Jesus in the mission of the church in the Acts of the Apostles. How could it be that one would rise from the dead and anyone still refuse to repent? There will be no special treatment for those who refuse the needs of the wretched at their gate. If they will not hear the scriptures and be merciful, then they show that they have placed themselves beyond the reach of God's mercy. By the end of the parable, the hearer's point of identification has become clear. The parable is addressed to "lovers of money" (16:14). At the beginning, hearers or readers may assume that they are expected to identify with the rich man or with Lazarus, but the parable is far more subtle. By the end of the parable, we realize that we stand in the place of the rich man's brothers. The question is whether we will hear the scriptures and repent.

Points for Reflection

Did the brothers ever get the message? We are not told, for that is the question the parable leaves us to answer. Each of us will write our own ending to the story.

In modern times, Lazarus corresponds to the person who begs, a panhandler. One dares not look into his or her eyes, lest a claim is made upon one's compassion. It is acceptable to give aid to the worthy poor, but it is socially permissible to regard some as unworthy. Whoever is attentive to the parable will also be attentive to the needs of both the economically and spiritually poor and respond with help.

The parable encourages more than charity. It exhorts the disciples of Jesus in every age to see the conditions of those who suffer and to see them as persons created in the image and likeness of God. While the poor among us may be silent, as Lazarus was in the parable, God speaks on their behalf to the rich and powerful.

Finally, the parable teaches abhorrence of the use of the poor for the gain of the rich, as the rich man tried to use Lazarus even after the rich man had died.

For Discussion

1. Describe what you think a fool is in the eyes of people, of Jesus and of God.

2. Do your possessions get in the way of your practice of faith? Where does your treasure lie?

3. What does it mean for you to be "rich toward God"?

4. What is your attitude toward the poor, the disenfranchised and the marginalized?

5. What role do greed and hedonism play in your life and in your relationships with others? Is it ever a stumbling block to the practice of faith?

Parables about Praying

"Lord, teach us to pray, . . ."

(Luke 11:1)

In the gospel of Luke, Jesus prays more often than he does in any other gospel. There are seven references to Jesus praying in Luke. He prays at every major transition in his life: at his baptism (3:21), when he retreats into the wilderness (5:16), when he chooses the apostles (6:12), as he starts his ministry in Gentile territory (9:18), at his transfiguration (9:28), when he teaches the disciples how to pray the "Our Father" (11:1) and during the agony in the garden (22:40–46). Prayer and Jesus as a man of prayer are central themes in the gospel of Luke.[1] The reader of Luke's gospel is challenged to live life as Jesus lived, praying at the crucial points in his or her life.

Chapter Eight

At the baptism of Jesus, Luke is the only gospel to say that Jesus was praying (3:21). His praying seems to continue through the descent of the Holy Spirit and the voice of God from heaven declaring Jesus his beloved son. This critical moment of calling and empowerment of Jesus by the Father takes place within the context of Jesus' prayerful communication with the Father.

Luke is careful to note that Jesus demonstrated a balance between his public ministry and his life of solitary prayer. The gospel reports that great crowds assembled to listen to the teaching of Jesus and to be cured of illness. However, Luke says Jesus "would withdraw to deserted places and pray" (5:16). The tense of the Greek verb meaning "to withdraw" suggests that the withdrawal of Jesus for prayer was a repeated action during his busy public life.

Another critical time of decision in Jesus' life was his choice of the twelve. These twelve are particularly important in Luke's narrative as the foundation of the restored Israel, which, for Luke, is the emerging church. They and their successors will continue the mission of Jesus to the ends of the earth (Acts of the Apostles). Before making this choice, the gospel says Jesus "went out to the mountain to pray; and he spent the night in prayer to God" (6:12). This selection of the twelve thus arises from Jesus' first withdrawal and communing with God. His praying on the mountain throughout the night enabled him to choose wisely and confidently.

A significant transition occurs in the gospel when Jesus questions his disciples concerning his identity. "Who do the crowds say I am? Who do you say I am?" (Luke 9:18–20). Luke sets this crucial question in the context of prayer: "Once when Jesus was praying alone, with only the disciples near him, he asked them" (9:18). Reflecting on the identity of Jesus and who he is in our lives is best done in quiet, reflective prayer. Solitary prayer while in the presence of the disciples seems to be a contradiction. Jesus could have been praying privately while his disciples were around him, or Jesus could have been praying with his disciples but away from the crowds. Jesus teaches us that we can withdraw for prayer either individually or with others. We do not have to be a hermit to find time for prayer.

The transfiguration of Jesus, like the scene of his baptism, is a moment of revelation in Luke's gospel. As he does with the revelation at Jesus' baptism, Luke situates the transfiguration in the context of prayer. Luke alone of all the gospels explicitly states that Jesus "went up on the mountain to pray" (9:28). The mountain is often the place of prayer in Luke, and here Jesus takes Peter, James and John to pray with him. The gospel says that the appearance of Jesus changed "while he was praying" (9:28–29). Luke is telling his readers that prayer must be the setting in which we also discern and discover who Jesus is and how he is transfigured before us and simultaneously transfigures our own lives.

In addition, Luke emphasizes that prayer was the context in which Jesus began and ended his passion. At the last supper, Jesus tells Peter, "I have prayed for you that your own faith may not fail" (22:32), as he foretells Peter's denial. Before his arrest, Jesus prays in agony to his Father, asking that the cup of suffering pass from him, but also surrendering himself to the Father's will (22:41–44). This prayer of Jesus on the Mount of Olives reveals the internal disposition of Jesus as he is about to die. Like Jacob wrestling through the night with the angel, this prayer of Jesus was a great struggle, so fervent that his perspiration became like drops of blood. Luke is the only gospel that uses the Greek word *agony* in this context; its meaning is derived from athletics, where it was the kind of exercise an athlete performed that resulted in profuse perspiration. The implication is that prayer requires the same strenuous exercise. At the end of his passion, the final words of Jesus are from Israel's book of prayer, the Psalms. "Father, into your hands I commend my spirit" (Luke 23:46; Psalm 31:5) is the prayer of Jesus from the cross as he breathes his last.

In Luke's gospel, the disciples must have seen Jesus go away for times of prayer several times. They saw how important prayer was for Jesus, and they saw how Jesus prayed in all the decision-making moments of his life. Jesus gave silent witness to the value of prayer, and it was this personal witness that inspired his disciples' request to teach them how to pray. Luke tells us that Jesus "was praying in a certain place and after he had finished, one of his disciples said to him, 'Lord, teach us to pray'" (11:1). Luke invites us, his readers, to go off with Jesus and to learn from him how to pray.

Jesus taught his disciples to pray as he prayed; he taught them the prayer we call the "Our Father" (11:1–4). The most important aspect of this prayer was to address God in prayer as Father. The Father of Jesus was to be the disciples' Father too. A disciple is privileged to call upon God as a loving parent with the same intimacy that Jesus has with God. The prayer Jesus taught is a model for all Christian prayer. It is simple and direct; it praises God, requests the basic needs of life and asks for God's forgiveness. It is the prayer the Christian community has continued to pray since the days of Jesus.

The Lord's Prayer in Luke is followed by the teachings of Jesus about prayer in the form of parables. It is to these parables that we now turn.

Luke's Parables on Prayer

The three parables on prayer in Luke are the parable of the friend at midnight (11:5–8), the parable of the persistent widow (18:1–8) and the parable of the Pharisee and the tax collector (18:9–14). They are masterfully told by Jesus and are profoundly challenging to anyone who encounters them. They provide meditations on prayer in the form of a story.

In exploring the first of these three parables on prayer, namely the friend at midnight (11:5–8), we will also look at the two parabolic sayings about asking, seeking and knocking (11:9–10) and about a child's request of his parent (11:11–13).

The Parable of the Friend at Midnight and Connected Parabolic Sayings

> [5]And he said to them, "Suppose one of you has a friend, and you go to him at midnight and say to him, 'Friend, lend me three loaves of bread; [6]for a friend of mine has arrived, and I have nothing to set before him.'

⁷And he answers from within, 'Do not bother me; the door has already been locked, and my children are with me in bed; I cannot get up and give you anything.' ⁸I tell you, even though he will not get up and give him anything because is he is his friend, at least because of his persistence he will get up and give him whatever he needs.

⁹"So I say to you, Ask, and it will be given you; search, and you will find; knock, and the door will be opened for you. ¹⁰For everyone who asks receives, and everyone who searches finds, and for everyone who knocks, the door will be opened. ¹¹Is there anyone among you who, if your child asks for a fish, will give a snake instead of a fish? ¹²Or if the child asks for an egg, will give a scorpion? ¹³If you then, who are evil, know how to give good gifts to your children, how much more will the heavenly Father give the Holy Spirit to those who ask him!" (Luke 11:5–13)

Luke has set this parable in the context of an extended presentation on prayer in 11:1–13. The emphasis is on the nature of the God to whom Christians pray. The first part, verses 1 through 4, contains the Lord's Prayer. Although Luke's placement and wording of the Lord's Prayer is different from Matthew's (6:9–13), a main point in common with Matthew's version is the use of the term "Father." This carries with it an assurance of the basis on which God will answer our prayers, that is, because he is a loving and caring parent. The portrayal of God in the second part of this section of chapter 11, in verses 5 through 8, is the parable itself.

The third part of chapter 11, verses 9 and 10, calls for action on the part of the petitioner: asking, seeking, knocking. But still the focus is not on the petitioner; it is on God who is faithful and consistent in his response. The petitioner could not be guaranteed an answer if God were not faithful. The fourth part (11:11–13) portrays the wisdom and kindness of a father who gives good gifts to his children.

The emphasis throughout this section is on God, who receives petitions in prayer and who will surely hear and answer. The first component, the Lord's Prayer, and the last component, the wise father, are linked by references to a father. The second component, the parable, and the third, the invitation to ask, seek and knock, have in common references to the petitioner taking the initiative and doing so with an expectation of an answer. Finally, the context of the parable (11:5–8) probably stems from the petition for daily bread (verse 3) in the Lord's Prayer.

This parable assumes the setting of a Galilean village. Houses were simple structures of one or two rooms. Women baked bread in ovens in common courtyards, so they would know who might have bread left at the end of the day. Hospitality was such a serious duty that any failure to provide for a guest would bring shame on the host and on his family.

The parable unfolds in one long question: "Which of you?" and it expects a negative answer: "No one. It would be unthinkable." The repetition of the word for friend, in Greek *philos*, makes friendship the underlying premise of the parable. The parable constructs a web of friendships: the hearer and his or her imagined friend, the one who goes to a friend's house in the middle of the night to ask for bread and the friend who arrives late as an unexpected guest. The two central characters in the parable can be designated as the *petitioner* and the *sleeper*. The *petitioner* has received a guest and is obliged to provide him with a meal. Presumably, there was other food in the house, but not the essential ingredient of the meal, bread, the staff of life. The parable then asks whether anyone could imagine the situation in which one would go to a friend in the middle of the night and be told by him that he could not get up to give the bread the *petitioner* needed because he and his family were asleep. To get up in the middle of the night, get the bread and draw the bolt on the door would awaken the whole family. Would a neighbor turn away a friend in the middle of the night and allow himself to be shamed because he would not provide hospitality for a guest? Such a thing would be unimaginable in the Galilean village. The situation is unthinkable not because of the *petitioner's* persistence, but because honor demanded that a neighbor get up, awaken his whole family if necessary and supply his friend's need—if not for friendship's sake, then at least to avoid being shamed.

The parable requires us to compare our expectations of a neighbor with our assumptions about God. If a neighbor would help us, would God be any slower to answer an urgent request? The neighbor might have to be roused from sleep but, as the psalmist says, God neither slumbers nor sleeps (Psalm 121:4). Luke is implying that we may pray confidently, therefore, not because we trust in our own persistence, but because we know that in a time of need God is even more trustworthy than any human neighbor.

Points for Reflection

The message this parable conveys to Jesus' disciples is that they could approach God confidently, even brashly, in a way that might offend the sensibilities of others. In a culture of honor and shame (the culture at the time of the gospel of Luke), what is at stake is not necessarily what is morally right or morally wrong, but rather what is acceptable or unacceptable among one's peers. The disciples can approach God in a shameless way, but they can do so only because God will "cover" for their shame when God acts in accordance with his own honor.[2]

As we read the parable today in its Lucan context, matters become even clearer. The Lord's Prayer begins with the request that God's name be honored. The Lord's Prayer also deals with the provision of bread for the day. So we can approach God knowing that we have already been invited to pray regarding God's honor as well as daily provisions. Furthermore, following the parable (verses 9–10) assures us that God will be consistent and faithful in responding to our asking, seeking and knocking. Then verses 11 through 13 show us that a human father

acts wisely and kindly as he responds to the requests of his children. Jesus compares the generosity of an earthly father with the generosity of God. The whole passage, therefore, is teaching us about God: He is a loving and gracious Father who will uphold his own honor and will not let us be ashamed when we pray; he is a wise and kind Father, consistent and faithful in his response.

Jesus' teachings on prayer, therefore, require that the one who prays will pray as one aware of desperate self-need before God. Jesus' parables and teachings assure us that prayer is effective not because of our cajoling or because we have found the right words, but because of God's nature as one who loves his own and wants to give to those in need. Prayer is where we bring our need to God's love in faith.

By means of the parable of the friend at midnight, Jesus teaches us to persist in prayer, but not because we have to convince God to answer us or to wear down God's resistance. Rather, Jesus teaches persistence to overcome our tendency to give up on prayer too easily or to pray too sporadically.

The Parable of the Persistent Widow

> [1]Then Jesus told them a parable about their need to pray always and not to lose heart. [2]He said, "In a certain city there was a judge who neither feared God nor had respect for people. [3]In that city there was a widow who kept coming to him and saying, 'Grant me justice against my opponent.' [4]For a while he refused; but later he said to himself, 'Though I have no fear of God and no respect for anyone, [5]yet because this widow keeps bothering me, I will grant her justice, so that she may not wear me out by continually coming.'" [6]And the Lord said, "Listen to what the unjust judge says. [7]And will not God grant justice to his chosen ones who cry to him day and night? Will he delay long in helping them? [8]I tell you, he will quickly grant justice to them. And yet, when the Son of Man comes, will he find faith on earth?" (Luke 18:1–8)

The force of this parable depends heavily on the social status and religious duties involved in the roles of judges and widows. In ancient Israel, the duty of a judge was to maintain harmonious relations and to arbitrate disputes between Israelites. Widows were deprived of the support of a husband, yet they couldn't inherit their husband's estate, which passed on to the deceased man's sons or brothers, so disputes involving widows and orphans were common. Judges were charged with the responsibility of hearing complaints fairly and impartially, a duty that was all the more important because they judged cases without the benefit of a jury. The judge's responsibility within the covenant community, therefore, was to declare God's judgment and establish *shalom*, peace, among God's people.

The expectation regarding the care of widows in the Hebrew Scriptures and in ancient Israel was equally clear. Regard for those in need—among whom the widow, the orphan and the foreigner were classic examples—was grounded in God's mercy on the Israelites when they were in bondage (Deuteronomy 24:17–18). God will vindicate the widows and the orphans. Therefore, those who abuse such powerless persons will surely suffer God's judgment (Exodus 22:22–24; Psalm 68:5).

Widows had a place of honor in the early church also. The epistle of James declares that "religion that is pure and undefiled before God, the Father, is this: to care for orphans and widows in their distress and to keep oneself unstained by the world" (1:27). The pastoral epistles document the church's effort to care for its widows and characterized the widow as one whose piety leads her to continual prayer: "The real widow, left alone, has set her hope on God and continues in supplications and prayers night and day" (1 Timothy 5:5).

In this light, the prominence of widows in Luke and Acts takes on an added significance. Anna, the widow who blessed the infant Jesus, "never left the temple but worshipped there with fasting and prayer night and day" (Luke 2:37). During his address at Nazareth at the outset of his ministry, Jesus recalled Elijah's ministry to the widow of Sidon (4:25–26). Elijah provided her with meal and oil and then revived her son and presented him to her alive (1 Kings 17:8–24). Jesus' raising of the widow of Nain's son in Luke 7:11–17 calls attention to the connections between Luke's account of that event and Elijah's resuscitation of the widow's son. Later, Luke will record Jesus' condemnation of those who "devour widows' houses" (20:47) and of the widow who put two copper coins in the treasury (21:1–3).

Jesus was aware of the plight of widows in his day. Unscrupulous persons, even members of their own family, could easily victimize them. Thus the picture of a widow seeking justice for herself would have been common enough for the creation of a parable. In order to instruct his followers on prayer, Jesus needed an illustration. He fastened on to this one to show that, if a wicked, rogue judge will help out a widow who keeps pestering him, surely God will respond to the needs of widows and all of his children who cry out to him.

In structure and theme, the parable of the widow and the judge, which is found only in the gospel of Luke, is a twin of the parable of the neighbor in need (11:5–8). Both are used to illustrate the importance of persistent prayer. Both parables feature a person in need persistently pressing a request, and both parables call for reasoning from the lesser to the greater: If a neighbor or an unjust judge will respond to an urgent or repeated request, then will not God also respond to those who call out in need?

Verse 1 serves as an introduction to the parable and instructs the reader to interpret it as a lesson on prayer: "Then Jesus told them a parable about their need to pray always and not to lose heart" (18:1). The parable continues by introducing a certain "judge" in a certain city. This situation is either hypothetical or deliberately non-specific. All attention is focused on the characterization of this judge, "who neither feared God nor had respect for people." In light of the requirements and expectations for judges mentioned earlier, the point is obvious—this judge is completely unfit for his position. The reader can have no confidence that the judge will execute justice or minister with compassion. The tension in the parable is created by the surprise that the judge does not act as we have been led to expect.

To "fear God" in this context may mean either to reverence God, namely holding God in awe, or to live in fear of punishment for violating his office as a judge. Both the gospel of Luke and the Acts of the Apostles emphasize fear of God in the sense consistent with the sage's words: "The fear of the Lord is the beginning of knowledge; fools despise wisdom and instruction" (Proverbs 1:7). God's mercy comes to those who fear God (Luke 1:50); the shepherds literally "feared a great fear" at the angelic announcement of Jesus birth (2:9). The disciples and others respond in fear to Jesus' power (8:25, 35, 9, 34, 45) and Jesus instructs the disciples not to fear the persecutors but to fear God—to hold God in awe (12:4–5). This judge, however, neither fears God nor respects people. Thus he could not be a faithful disciple by Lucan standards.

Interestingly enough, when the parable introduces the widow, her grievance is not described. However, it is assumed she is calling upon the judge to make a third party give her what is owed to her, possibly money or property. Neither does the parable tell us why the judge refuses to hear her case, but his refusal to hear it confirms Jesus' characterization as one who has no fear of God or regard for others. We may assume that the widow has a legitimate grievance. The judge is her sole hope of securing justice and persistence is her only recourse.

Luke provides an element of surprise in the judge's interior monologue. Interior monologues are a favored device in those parables unique to the gospel of Luke. See the monologue in the parables of the rich fool, 12:17–19; the prodigal son, 15:17–19; and the dishonest steward, 16:3–4. We are not actually told that the judge granted the widow's request, only that he decided to do so. The judge's soliloquy repeats Jesus' characterization of him. The judge will grant the widow's request for two reasons, but the statement of the second reason may be understood either literally or metaphorically. The language is drawn from the boxing arena. Literally it means, "so that in the end she may not come and strike me under the eye," that is, slap him or strike him in the face.[3] The expression can also be understood metaphorically to mean "so that she may not wear me out by continually coming." The metaphorical sense is preferred in modern English translations of the Bible.

The unjust judge, from whom one could hardly expect justice, finally does what is right, if only to keep from being badgered by the persistent widow. The interpretation of the parable begins with the admonition to consider what the unjust judge says. But what is the meaning of this brief story? If one focuses on the unjust judge, the point may be the contrast between the unjust judge and the character of God, who serves as a just judge over Israel.[4]

If even an unjust human judge will heed the widow and do what is right, how much more so will God do justice for the poor and the oppressed? On the other hand, a lesson on prayer emerges when one considers the widow's persistence in coming to the judge. Here, the emphasis may fall either on the importance of praying persistently, earnestly and without losing heart, the point with which Luke introduces the parable (18:1), or on the assurance that God will answer those who pray day and night.

Points for Reflection

To every reader in every age, the parable of the unjust judge and the persistent widow calls for reexamination of one's practice of faith. The parable is also a call to conversion. This challenge is succinctly stated by Megan McKenna:

Everyone is called to conversion in the parable, no matter who we think we are in the story or who God is. Whether we are the judge or the opponent, eventually God is going to get us, according to the story, and when he does he will bring swift, thorough and powerful justice in the name of the poor, the orphan, the widowed, the illegal alien, the stranger and foreigner in our midst.[5]

Have we turned a deaf ear to those who cry out in need, or have we given up hope that God will hear our calls for help? Faith requires different responses from the widow and the judge. What does faith require of us? Do we have the faith and persistence of the widow? The church and all of its members are reminded by this parable and its application not only of the need to be persistent in prayer, but also to be accountable in justice.

Finally, the parable challenges all who read it and pray with, through and in it not to lose heart in prayer. It is easy to lose heart in prayer, especially when we feel our prayers are not answered. Yet God may be answering in a way that is different from our expectations and which demands that we ponder this in our hearts.

The Parable of the Pharisee and the Tax Collector

[9]He also told this parable to some who trusted in themselves that they were righteous and regarded others with contempt: [10]"Two men went up to the temple to pray, one a Pharisee and the other a tax collector. [11]The Pharisee, standing by himself, was praying thus, 'God, I thank you that I am not like other people: thieves, rogues, adulterers, or even like this tax collector. [12]I fast twice a week; I give a tenth of all my income.'" [13]But the tax collector, standing far off, would not even look up to heaven, but was beating his breast and saying, 'God, be merciful to me, a sinner!' [14]I tell you, this man went down to his home justified rather than the other; for all who exalt themselves will be humbled, but all who humble themselves will be exalted." (Luke 18:9–14)

Luke adds this story to his depiction of many forms of prayer. He has shown Mary (1:46–55), Simeon (2:29–32), Anna (2:38) and Jesus (10:21–22) praying in thanksgiving. Prayers of praise have been offered by Zechariah (1:67–79), the heavenly host (2:13–14) and shepherds (2:20). Jesus has taught his disciples intercessory prayer, the Our Father (11:1–4). Jesus has instructed his followers to pray even for their enemies (6:28) and exemplifies it with his profound prayer for forgiveness for those who crucify him (23:34). To this portrait, Luke now adds the humble prayer of the tax collector who knows his need for God's mercy. A tax collector, despised by others and expected to be despised by God, exemplifies the healthy posture of prayer: seeking mercy from God who is the source of all mercy. We are immediately reminded of the Psalms: "The Lord is gracious and merciful" (Psalm 111:4; Psalm 145:8) and Deuteronomy 4:31: "The Lord your God is a merciful God."

Luke says that Jesus told the parable "to some who trusted in themselves that they were righteous and regarded others with contempt" (verse 18). Both facets of this description anticipate the characterization of the Pharisee in the following verses. While the parable may be intended as a rebuke of the Pharisees in the present context, Luke does not say that Jesus addressed the Pharisees. Moreover, a parable addressed to the Pharisees that placed them in an unfavorable light would hardly be subtle; thus the parable probably has a much wider application. Disciples are just as vulnerable to pride and self-righteousness as the Pharisees. While those who do not recognize their own tendency to play the role of the Pharisee in this parable may assume that Jesus was talking about others, by the end of the story readers will have to confront the attitude of the Pharisee in their own hearts. Such an interpretation avoids anti-Semitism. The conclusion disallows the limitation of the parable to any one group: "All who exalt themselves will be humbled, but all who humble themselves will be exalted" (18:14).

Trusting in oneself is a posture of blindness to one's position before God. Like the strong man who trusted in his armor in Luke 11:21–22, the religiously observant may trust in their righteousness. Luke takes pains, however, to identify the true basis for righteousness and distinguish it from misplaced pride in obedience to God's commandments. Zechariah and Elizabeth were righteous (1:6). John's role, likewise, was to turn the disobedient to the wisdom of the righteous (1:17), of whom Simeon was an appropriate model (2:25). Alongside these models of piety were others whose righteousness was superficial or inadequate. Jesus came, therefore, "to call not the righteous but sinners to repentance" (5:32). This ambivalence continues in other references. The righteous will be raised from the dead (14:14), but there is more joy in heaven over the repentance of one sinner than in 99 righteous (15:7). Later, Jesus' accusers will feign righteousness (20:20) but the centurion at the cross will pronounce Jesus righteous (23:47) and Joseph of Arimathea, who buries the body of Jesus, will be identified as a righteous man (23:50).

Valuable as the introduction and conclusion may be, they may rob the parable of much of its subtlety and reduce its characters to stereotypes. The parable itself characterizes the Pharisee and the tax collector only indirectly; it does not tell us what to think of them. The parable leaves it to the hearer to decide why one was justified and the other was not. The open-ended nature of the parable requires the hearer/reader to make a judgment.

With great literary ability, Luke reports both the position and prayer of the Pharisee and that of the tax collector, and the reader learns who these two are by the way they pray. The Pharisees separated themselves from others to maintain their purity before God, so this Pharisee takes a position that reflects his identity—standing by himself. Alternatively, the phrase may be interpreted as referring to the Pharisee's prayer rather than his position. It can be translated: "Concerning himself he prayed these things." Both prayers begin with a simple direct address: "God." The Pharisee's prayer, however, continues immediately in the *first person*. The narrator's initial characterization of the Pharisee regarding others with contempt is confirmed by his own words. His prayer is one of thanksgiving but it is a self-serving prayer, thanking God that he is not like other people. By "other people" he means sinners: "thieves, rogues, adulterers, or even like this tax collector" (18:11). The last member of this list links the two characters of the parable. The Pharisee is aware of the presence of the tax collector in the temple, but the only link between them is the Pharisee's contempt for the other.

As the Pharisee's prayer continues, so does his absorption in his own virtue. Fasting and tithing are the proofs of his piety that he offers to God. The Pharisee does not just offer a tithe on those foods and animals for which a tithe is specifically required; he tithes all of his income. The Pharisee asks nothing of God. He presumes, rather, that he is not a sinner and that his fasting and tithing are ample evidence of his piety. The Pharisee gives no evidence of either humility or contrition before God.

In contrast, the tax collector stands "far off" and in a position that anticipates his confession of unworthiness before God. The common posture for prayer in Jesus' day and at the time of the writing of Luke's gospel was not on one's knees with head bowed and hands folded, but rather standing upright and looking up to God with hands raised. Indeed, later Christian prayer practices reflect the influence of this parable. Beating one's breast was a sign of remorse or grief. The parable makes it clear that in 18:13 the Pharisee asks nothing of God. Nor does he boast of anything. His prayer echoes the opening words of Psalm 51: "Have mercy on me, O God." The crucial addition to the words of Psalm 51, however, is the tax collector's self-designation: "a sinner." Nothing more is reported of the tax collector's prayer. It is complete as it stands and nothing more needs to be said of his character.

Points for Reflection

Luke has educated the reader to know how to assess the contrast between the two who went up to the temple to pray. Early in his ministry, Jesus said, "I have come to call not the righteous but sinners to repentance" (5:32). The parable now contrasts representatives from each of these categories. Jesus' opponents ridiculed him as "a friend of tax collectors and sinners" (7:34), but Jesus responded that "there will be more joy in heaven over one sinner who repents than over ninety-nine righteous persons who need no repentance" (15:7).

Less evident is the reason why the Pharisee's prayer is not accepted. Is it because he presumes he is righteous but is not? Does his lack of humility or his confidence in his own virtue exclude him from God's grace? Does the fact that he has separated himself from others signal that, although he may not realize it, he has separated himself from God as well? While the parable elicits these questions, it does not answer them—the reader is left to consider the contrast between the two characters. The parable is not merely a study in contrasts, therefore, but a dramatic call to examine one's own conscience.

The parable of the Pharisee and the tax collector is a two-sided parable. To read it as simply a warning against pride, self-sufficiency or a relationship with God based on one's own works is to miss the other side of the parable, which connects the Pharisee's posture before God with his contempt for the tax collector. To miss this connection would be tantamount to emulating the Pharisee's blindness to the implications of his attitude toward the tax collector. The nature of grace is paradoxical: It can be received only by those who have learned empathy for others. In that regard, grace partakes of the nature of mercy and forgiveness. Only the merciful can receive mercy and only those who forgive will be forgiven (Luke 6:36–38). The Pharisee was religious enough to be virtuous but not enough to be humble. As a result, his religion drove him away from the tax collector rather than toward him.

One final twist on the parable seems to be that readers are invited to emulate the tax collector, who is usually seen as a sympathetic and falsely maligned figure. Instinctively, readers despise the Pharisee, who is seen as despising all other human beings. But perhaps the parable invites us to see how, by the very act of judging the Pharisee, we ourselves are exemplifying the judgmental attitude we despise in him. From this position, there is no smugness of superiority toward any other. All are seen as brothers and sisters of the same gracious God.[6]

Luke's parables on prayer are a veritable examination of conscience, for they require the reader to ponder how the behavior of the various characters impinges on the reader. What remains constant throughout is that God is always open to hear prayer. Furthermore, prayer requires work and effort on the part of the believer. It requires persistence and excludes presumption.

For Discussion

1. Do you pray? Do you believe God hears your prayers?

2. Do you ever pray with or from the Bible? If so, how does it help your prayer life?

3. Is Jesus, as he is portrayed in the gospel of Luke, a model for your prayer life? Do you pray in your life as often as Jesus prayed in his life?

4. Are you persistent in your prayer? Is persistence a needed virtue for prayer?

5. How does reflecting on the characters of the widow, the Pharisee and the tax collector help you to reflect on your own prayer life?

Parables about Forgiveness, Table Fellowship and Compassion

"Then Peter came and said to him, 'Lord,
if another member of the church sins against me,
how often should I forgive?'"

(Matthew 18:21)

This chapter will offer reflections on three parables. The first centers around the theme of God's forgiveness. It is usually called "the parable of the unforgiving slave," but it could just as easily be named "the parable of God's extraordinary forgiveness" (Matthew 18:23–35). The second is the parable of the great banquet (Luke 14:7–14), which deals with table fellowship. The third is possibly the best known of Jesus' parables, even by people who never read the Bible, the parable of the good Samaritan (Luke 10:25–37). These three are being considered together here, for in a way they are lenses through which God can be viewed as forgiving, inclusive and compassionate.

Chapter Nine

The Parable of the Unforgiving Slave

[23]"For this reason the kingdom of heaven may be compared to a king who wished to settle accounts with his slaves. [24]When he began the reckoning, one who owed him ten thousand talents was brought to him; [25]and, as he could not pay, his lord ordered him to be sold, together with his wife and children and all his possessions, and payment to be made. [26]So the slave fell on his knees before him, saying, 'Have patience with me, and I will pay you everything.' [27]And out of pity for him, the lord of that slave released him and forgave him the debt. [28]But that same slave, as he went out, came upon one of his fellow slaves who owed him a hundred denarii; and seizing him by the throat, he said, 'Pay what you owe.' [29]Then his fellow slave fell down and pleaded with him, 'Have patience with me, and I will pay you.' [30]But he refused; then he went and threw him into prison until he would pay the debt. [31]When his fellow slaves saw what had happened, they were greatly distressed and they went and reported to their lord all that had taken place. [32]Then his lord summoned him and said to him, 'You wicked slave! I forgave you all that debt because you pleaded with me. [33]Should you not have had mercy on your fellow slave, as I had mercy on you?' [34]And in anger his lord handed him over to be tortured until he would pay his entire debt. [35]So my heavenly Father will also do to every one of you, if you do not forgive your brother or sister from your heart." (Matthew 18:23–35)

This parable appears only in the gospel of Matthew. It consists of three main parts plus an application at the end. The first part concerns the king's dealings with his slave (18:23–27); the second concerns the slave's dealings with his fellow slaves (18:28–31); the third concerns the king's dealing with his slave once more in light of what has happened (18:32–34). The final verse is an application.

Any interpretation of the parable has to look at the meaning of the term *talent*. The slave owes the king 10,000 talents, a truly astronomical figure. The term *talent* referred to a monetary amount equivalent to 6,000 denarii.[1] Since a denarius was a day's wages for a common laborer, and he might work some 300 days per year, a talent would be worth nearly twenty years' wages. The amount owed by the slave would be equivalent to nearly 200,000 years' wages for one man or a year's wages for 200,000 persons.[2] It is precisely the fantastic size of the debt that makes the parable so memorable.

The amount owed is ridiculously high. What slave could ever accumulate such a debt owed to a king? It is doubtful that even Herod the Great, certainly one of the richest persons of Jesus' day, could have paid such a debt. Frequently, parables contain hyperbole and humor, displaying actions that are surprising and outlandish, as this one does here and as it will again when the king forgives the debt.

In addition, there may be some hyperbole surrounding the king's orders to sell the man and his family for the debt he owes. According to the Torah, a man can be sold as a slave if he cannot make restitution for theft (Exodus 22:1), and there are other Hebrew Scripture passages referring to the sale of children as slaves for the debts of their deceased father (2 Kings 4:1) or to pay off debts during times of famine (Nehemiah 5:5). But there are no legal grounds in Jewish law for the sale of a man in debt. Nevertheless, Palestine was under Roman rule, and the kings known to the hearers of the parable were not observant Jews. Parables that have kings as major figures within them, whether they are parables of Jesus or of the rabbis, can be expected to portray kings in ways that popular imagination supposed they would act. As stock characters, they are typically wealthy, powerful and ruthless. That is what kings are supposed to be; if they were not described that way, the storyteller would use a figure other than a king.

The modern reader often raises other questions about this parable: How would the sale of the slave and his family into the hands of another master lead to the repayment of the debt? Or why couldn't the debtor pay at least part of his debt and be on good terms? Some questions are simply out of order in listening to or reading a parable. Often by asking them, one ruins a good story.

As the parable proceeds, the king cancels the slave's debt. The slave is not simply given an extension, which is all he had asked for; rather, he is forgiven the entire debt. Metaphors abound in this parable. The king is a metaphor for God, as elsewhere in the parables of Jesus (Matthew 22:2–14; 25:31–46) and often in rabbinic parables. The debt is a metaphor for sin. The first slave metaphorically equals the one who is forgiven an enormous debt of sin by God; the second slave metaphorically equals the one who has committed an ordinary sin against a fellow human being or a fellow Christian. The challenge of the parable is for Christians to forgive one another as God forgives them.

In the parable, the debt of the fellow slave is 100 denarii, equal to about four months' wages (figuring twenty-four work days per month, if the laborer was a Jew who observed the Sabbath). The ratio of difference between the two debts would, therefore, have been immense, roughly 600,000 to 1. (The first slave's debt of 10,000 talents would equal 60,000,000 denarii—one talent equals 6,000 denarii—which is 600,000 times more than his fellow slaves' debt of 100 denarii.)

The refusal of the first slave to practice compassion toward his fellow slave is quick, and retaliation is decisive. Putting his fellow slave in prison for debt was an act forbidden by Jewish law from ancient times, but it was a widespread custom allowed by Greco-Roman law in the first century. The first slave's act toward his fellow slave was swift indeed. One would normally expect a court procedure prior to imprisonment (see Matthew 5:25–26; Luke 12:58–59), which is not mentioned here, but such details need not impede the progress of a parable.

Having refused forgiveness to his fellow slave, the king (God) now addresses the first slave as "wicked slave" (18:23–33). His wickedness is based on the fact that he had been the recipient of mercy and should have extended mercy to his fellow slave. As a result, the king hands him over to be dealt with severely. The slave has lost not only the forgiveness that he had received; the debt was back on his shoulders and he was facing torture. In any case, since there was no possibility of paying his debt of ten thousand talents he would be tortured as long as he lived. The closing verse of the parable (18:35) makes an application and the point of comparison is made as explicit as possible. Since God has forgiven the disciples so lavishly, they ought to forgive others in the same way.

Points for Reflection

The teaching of this parable is nuanced. Surely the parable does not teach that forgiving others is a prerequisite or means for gaining God's forgiveness. If human forgiveness is a precondition for divine forgiveness, no one can ever be forgiven by God. Human forgiveness is never perfect. One must always rely on the mercy of God, even when one's best efforts to forgive have been made. The parable and its application seek to move the disciple/reader to forgive: You have been forgiven so much, how can you not forgive the other person?

Since the parable deals with the forgiver (God) and the forgiven (a sinner), it is necessary first to realize that God's actions surpass all ways of human acting by far. What does the king do when the man pleads for more time? He says in effect, "Ah, forget it. You don't have to pay me back." The slave who gets off lightly is a scoundrel. He will not forgive as he himself has been forgiven.

The slave who will not forgive potentially represents the hearer and reader of the parable. As one who has been forgiven so much by God, a disciple of Jesus cannot be stingy in forgiving others. Unless one is ready to forgive others as God forgives, that person is like the slave who refuses to forgive his fellow slave.

Forgiveness is expected of a disciple of Jesus. The message of the parable is clear. To live well means to live with a generous and forgiving heart. The assumption behind all of it, however, is the extraordinary gospel of God's compassion and mercy.

The Parable of the Great Banquet

[15]One of the dinner guests, on hearing this, said to him, "Blessed is anyone who will eat bread in the kingdom of God!" [16]Then Jesus said to him, "Someone gave a great dinner and invited many. [17]At the time for the dinner he sent his slave to say to those who had been invited, 'Come; for everything is ready now.' [18]But they all alike began to make excuses. The first said to him, 'I have bought a piece of land, and I must go out and see it; please accept my regrets.' [19]Another said, 'I have bought five yoke of oxen, and I am going to try them out; please accept my regrets.' [20]Another said, 'I have just been married, and therefore I cannot come.' [21]So the slave returned and reported this to his master. Then the owner of the house became angry and said to his slave, 'Go out at once into the streets and lanes of the town and bring in the poor, the crippled, the blind, and the lame.' [22]And the slave said, 'Sir, what you ordered has been done, and there is still room.' [23]Then the master said to the slave, 'Go out into the roads and lanes and compel people to come in, so that my house may be filled. [24]For I tell you, none of those who were invited will taste my dinner.'" (Luke 14:15–24)

The gospel of Luke, more than any other gospel, stresses both Jesus' table fellowship with sinners and other marginal members of society (see Luke 5:29; 7:33–34; 36–50, 15:1) as well as meals as a setting for Jesus' teaching (see Luke

5:31–39; 7:36–50; 10:38–42; 11:37–52; 14:1–24; 22:14–38; 24:20–49). Meals were also a context for philosophical discussions in Greco-Roman literature. For example, the philosophers Plato and Plutarch refer to the *symposium,* which became, in effect, a literary form; the eating and drinking provided only the context for sometimes serious and sometimes frivolous discussions of life.[3] The fullest expression of this form is found in chapter 14 of Luke. The parable of the great dinner is part of the dinner conversation after the meal, which is cast like a Greco-Roman symposium. This would have made eminent sense to Luke's audience. It is part of Luke's presentation of Jesus as a philosopher as well as a prophet to have him conversing so often at table.

The banquet parable can also be situated against the backdrop of the image of a banquet for end-time feasting and celebration of God's ultimate triumph over evil as depicted by the prophet Isaiah: "On this mountain the Lord of hosts will make for all peoples a feast of rich food, a feast of well-aged wines, of rich food filled with marrow, of well aged wines strained clear" (Isaiah 25:6). Luke may have had this Isaiah text in mind as he conveyed the parable to his audience. If this is the case, then the parable is echoing a teaching found elsewhere in the gospel: "Blessed is anyone who will eat bread in the kingdom of God" (14:15; see 14:1).

In analyzing this parable, it is customary to look at its context. Chapter 14 of Luke is often described as the banquet discourse, in which Jesus shatters boundaries. It begins with Jesus not only healing a man with dropsy but doing so on the Sabbath (14:1–6). Jesus then vehemently criticizes taking positions of honor at meals that perpetuate social barriers and urges hosts to invite not their friends, but the poor, the crippled, the lame and the blind (14:7–14). The parable of the great supper follows (14:15–24). This is an image of the type of banquet that the faith community (church) is to hold when it celebrates a meal, most likely the eucharist. The table fellowship of Luke's church is to include those normally excluded by both social status and ritual law.

Excuses: Thanks but No Thanks

Attention should be drawn to the excuses offered by the first group that was invited. They offer three excuses: "I have bought a piece of land and I must go out and see it" (14:18); "I have bought five yoke of oxen and I am going to try them out" (14:19); and "I have just been married and therefore I cannot come" (14:20). These excuses can easily be justified on the basis of how a man can be excused from military service during a holy war, as described in Deuteronomy 20:5–7:

> [5]Then the officials shall address the troops, saying, "Has anyone built a new house but not dedicated it? He should go back to his house, or he might die in the battle and another dedicate it. [6]Has anyone planted a vineyard but not yet enjoyed its fruit? He should go back to his house, or he might die in the battle and another be first to enjoy its fruit. [7]Has anyone

become engaged to a woman but not yet married her? He should go back to his house, or he might die in the battle and another marry her."

Furthermore, Deuteronomy 24:5 clearly exempts a newly married male from having to do military service for one full year. "When a man is newly married, he shall not go out with the army or be charged with any related duty. He shall be free at home one year, to be happy with the wife whom he has married" (Deuteronomy 24:5).

Granting that such excuses apply to war, they do not apply to the banquet invitation. The excuses offered are obviously flimsy. When someone purchases a field, he looks it over long before he completes the transaction. The same is true when buying oxen. And the bridegroom was not asked to go to war but to dinner. The excuses both insult the host and convey to him the fact that he is being shunned by the guests he has invited.

Undaunted by the rebuff, the host invites the marginalized: the poor, the crippled, the blind and the lame (14:21). When he still has room for more guests, the host asks his slave to compel people to come in. This is most likely because peasants would not freely entertain going to the rich man's home, for they would be crossing the enormous chasm separating them. But the storyteller wants them to know the boundaries of society have been broken by Jesus' table fellowship.

The first invited guests, who will not taste the dinner in Luke's version (14:24), must be understood as the Pharisees and lawyers who actively reject Jesus. This is not a parable of the rejection of the Jews as such, because the "poor, blind, lame" who come into the banquet are themselves Jews, regardless of how they may have been marginalized. It is a parable of rejection told to the specific religious leaders and intended for them. It would be a flagrant error to equate the invitees who refuse to come to the banquet with the Jewish people as a whole. We are always challenged to avoid anti-Semitism whenever interpreting Sacred Scripture.

Points for Reflection

It is good to note that none of the guests invited to the banquet is kept away by something intrinsically evil or sinful—they simply make excuses. Others would give anything to have the opportunity that these declined.

The parable challenges readers of every walk of life to examine their consciences about excuses. Excuses can be deadly. They have the potential to poison the life of the Christian because they block the path to forgiveness and can rob faith of its vitality. The most dangerous excuses are those with which we fool ourselves. How often has our excuse been, "I have no time," or "I am too tired" or "I will get to it"? One of the most profound characteristics of excuses is that they simultaneously accuse as well as excuse because they reveal our true priorities. The excuses we offer to one another and to God reveal the activities and commitments we hold to be of greater importance.

Only those who dare to put aside their excuses can ever know the joy, peace, blessing and thrill of living by faith. The Lord is giving a party. The menu is food for the life of the spirit. We are all invited! Come to the feast!

The Parable of the Compassionate Samaritan

25Just then a lawyer stood up to test Jesus. "Teacher," he said, "what must I do to inherit eternal life?" 26He said to him, "What is written in the law? What do you read there?" 27He answered, "You shall love the Lord your God with all your heart, and with all your soul, and with all your strength, and with all your mind; and your neighbor as yourself." 28And he said to him, "You have given the right answer; do this, and you will live."

29But wanting to justify himself, he asked Jesus, "And who is my neighbor?" 30Jesus replied, "A man was going down from Jerusalem to Jericho, and fell into the hands of robbers, who stripped him, beat him, and went away, leaving him half dead. 31Now by chance a priest was going down that road; and when he saw him, he passed by on the other side. 32So likewise a Levite, when he came to the place and saw him, passed by on the other side. 33But a Samaritan while traveling came near him; and when he saw him, he was moved with pity. 34He went to him and bandaged his wounds, having poured oil and wine on them. Then he put him on his own animal, brought him to an inn, and took care of him. 35The next day he took out two denarii, gave them to the innkeeper, and said, 'Take care of him; and when I come back, I will repay you whatever more you spend.' 36Which of these three, do you think, was a neighbor to the man who fell into the hands of the robbers?" 37He said, "The one who showed him mercy." Jesus said to him, "Go and do likewise." (Luke 10:25–37)

Of all the parables of Jesus, it is fair to say that the story of the compassionate (or "good") Samaritan is one of the best known, equaled only, perhaps, by the prodigal son. The phrase "good Samaritan" has become such a part of the English language that many states have "good Samaritan" laws to protect people who help strangers in dire situations. Since the gospel of Luke does not give the parable a name, it will be referred to here as the parable of the compassionate Samaritan (Luke 10:25–37).

The parable is found only in the gospel of Luke. It is not to be taken as an account of an actual event that Jesus recalls. Rather, it is an artful creation by a master storyteller.

Vocabulary of the Parable

Since the parable of the compassionate Samaritan makes use of a variety of terms not immediately clear to a contemporary reader, let us explore them before going on to interpret the parable.

The term *lawyer* refers to an expert in the law. It refers to that type of professional who is sometimes called a "scribe" in other contexts, that is, a person who is trained to interpret and teach the law of Jewish tradition.

Normally, at the time of Jesus, the term *neighbor* would refer to a fellow Jew or proselyte. In asking the question about his neighbor, the lawyer is not seeking information (as in a definition), but to justify, or vindicate, himself. If Jesus agreed with the lawyer's limitation of the word *neighbor* to mean fellow Jews, it would eliminate the need to tell the parable.

The *road to Jericho* needs some explanation. Jesus narrates a story of a man going down from Jerusalem to Jericho. But why Jericho? Jesus chose this city as the man's destination because the road to it was known to be a treacherous and dangerous route. According to Flavius Josephus, a first century historian, the Jericho Road was "desolate and rocky," and when the Jews traveled it, they carried arms to protect themselves from robbers.[4] Anyone, even today, who has taken the road from Jerusalem to Jericho can attest that one "goes down" from Jerusalem to Jericho. The city of Jerusalem is some 2,700 feet above sea level; Jericho is 820 feet below sea level. That means there is a drop of over 3,500 feet, and the drop takes place within a 17-mile stretch of road.

Finally, one needs to understand that Jews did not associate with *Samaritans*. The origins of the Samaritans can be traced back to 722 BCE, when the northern kingdom of Israel had its capital at Samaria and was conquered by the Assyrians. The king of Assyria brought immigrants from foreign lands who worshipped foreign gods to live in Samaria. Over time the Jewish inhabitants intermarried with the immigrants, and, in the eyes of the Jewish people—especially those of Jesus' day—departed from Jewish customs and sensibilities regarding the law (see 2 Kings 17:24–41). Rejecting the Hebrew Scriptures as a whole, the Samaritans' only scriptures were a particular editing of the five books of Moses, the "Samaritan Pentateuch." Furthermore, they had their own temple at Mount Gerizim (John 4:9). The Samaritans were typically regarded as Gentiles, or—at best—a degree closer to Jews than the Gentiles, but still not full members of the house of Israel. "From the standpoint of Jews, the Samaritans were of Gentile extraction."[5]

Thus, by having a Samaritan as the one who helps the man in need, Jesus breaks down the boundaries between Jew and Samaritan, and between Jew and Gentile, but most of all he makes the claim that whoever responds to human needs is his disciple, a true child of God and an example of love for one's neighbor.

An Analysis of the Parable

A lawyer stood up to test Jesus. "Teacher," he said, "what must I do to inherit eternal life?" (10:25). It is important to be clear about what the lawyer is asking. He was *not* asking, "How can I get to heaven after I die?" Rather, the question about inheriting eternal life is a question about having a share in the coming of God's new age. It is a question about God's new reign. It is a question dealing with resurrection from the dead: "[Some] shall awake, some to everlasting life and some to shame and everlasting contempt" (Daniel 12:2).

Ultimately, then, the lawyer's question was a question about the sort of reign that Jesus was inaugurating. Is it one where eternal life and inheritance in land is rooted in God's Torah? Is it one that fulfills the eschatological hope of a new covenant with God's people Israel? Is Jesus really proclaiming something that is consistent with God's promises to Israel? These are the kinds of questions the lawyer is asking.

Unlike the other places where the question "What must I do to inherit eternal life?" is asked in Luke's gospel and answered by Jesus (18:18), here Jesus turns the question back on the lawyer. Jesus asks him, "What is written in the law? What do you read there?" (18:26). The lawyer answers by quoting the *Shema:* "Hear, O Israel: The Lord is our God, the Lord alone. You shall love the Lord your God with all your heart and with all your soul and with all your strength and with all your might" (Deuteronomy 6:4–5). Then he adds a quotation from Leviticus 19:18: "You shall love your neighbor as yourself" (10:27). "You have given the right answer," Jesus says. "Do this and you will live" (10:28). The lawyer has his answer: The reign of God that Jesus proclaims is one firmly rooted in the Hebrew Scriptures and the law of Israel.

But the lawyer doesn't stop there. He takes the matter a step further. "Wishing to justify himself, he said to Jesus, 'And who is my neighbor?'" Why would this lawyer wish to be justified? In first-century Judaism and indeed throughout the biblical tradition, it is the righteous, the justified ones, who will participate in God's new age. It is the righteous who will enter the kingdom; it is the righteous who will inherit eternal life. So the question of whether the lawyer is righteous or justified is closely linked to his first one of how to inherit eternal life.

The question of who should be accepted as a neighbor resulted in heated discussions in first-century Judaism. According to most mainstream texts of the time, the concept of *neighbor* should definitely include one's fellow Jews, but not necessarily go beyond that. In fact, the book of Sirach (12:1–7) not only makes it clear that one's help should not extend beyond the bounds of the Jewish people, but definitely not to "sinners" (that is, Gentiles), since to help sinners would be to condone their sins.

The question was not only a very real one in first-century Judaism, but it also had certain expected answers. Jesus, however, responds to the lawyer's question in an unexpected way. He tells a parable which begins in this way: "A man was going down from Jerusalem to Jericho and fell into the hands of robbers, who stripped him, beat him and went away, leaving him half dead" (10:30). The unnamed man never speaks during the whole parable, and we are not told if the man was Jewish. All we are told is that he fell into the hands of robbers (the Greek noun can also be translated "highwaymen" or "bandits"), with quite disastrous results.

Here the plot thickens: "Now by chance a priest was going down that road; and when he saw him, he passed by on the other side. So likewise a Levite, when he came to the place and saw him, passed on the other side" (10:31–32). There are good reasons why such behavior on the part of the priest might not have surprised Jesus' hearers. In order to accept the people's offerings and offer sacrifice in the temple, a priest was not to come in contact with a corpse. The man in the ditch was most likely unconscious. This means that there was no real way to tell if he were Jewish or even if he were still alive.

According to the Torah, contact with a corpse resulted in the most serious type of ritual uncleanness that one could contract. It took seven days to purify oneself from the uncleanness of a corpse, with the burning of a red heifer being required as part of the process (see Numbers 19). A priest, in fact, was not to defile himself with a corpse, except in the case of the death of his mother, father, son, daughter, brother, or virgin sister (see Leviticus 21:1–4). It was most likely, then, that this priest would take the most prudent path. For if this man turned out to be dead, his temple service would have been impossible to carry out.

Similar concerns hold for the Levite, whose task was to accept tithes from the people (see Nehemiah 10:37–38). Touching a corpse would also have made him ritually unclean and so prohibited him from temple service until he could have completed the seven-day ceremony for purification.

Jesus told this story in a context where there was considerable tension between Jewish peasants and the priesthood and temple aristocracy in Jerusalem.[6] His portrayal of the actions of the priest and the Levite would have served to confirm the animosity his listeners already had toward the clergy and aristocracy in Jerusalem. On a social level, therefore, the point could be easily drawn: The priest and the Levite did not help; they do not concern themselves with the plight of the peasants at any time.

In such a context it is clear where the story should go next. Since there are three traditional divisions among Jews (priests, Levites and all of Israel), the hero should have been a Jewish peasant, a faithful Israelite, who was traveling next on the road and, in spite of his lack of personal resources, helped the man who was robbed, beaten and left to die by the bandits. But in his own inimitable fashion, the Lucan Jesus completely overturns the expectations of his hearers. The next person to come along is a Samaritan.

As mentioned earlier, animosity between Jews and Samaritans was virulent, and it went both ways. Jews classed Samaritans in the same category as Philistines and Edomites (see Sirach 50:25–26). They had been accused in Jewish tradition of secretly entering Jerusalem during a Passover season and defiling the temple by strewing human bones "in the porticoes and throughout the temple."[7] And within the narrative of Luke's gospel, the Samaritans have already rejected Jesus at the outset of his journey to Jerusalem (see Luke 9:53). So by introducing a Samaritan into the story, Jesus was probably picking out a person who was considered by his audience to be one of the most odious characters possible. It would be like an African American storyteller selecting a member of the Ku Klux Klan as a hero for a story.

It is, therefore, all the more striking that Jesus goes on to describe the Samaritan in ways that could only have heightened the offensive nature of the story for his immediate audience. In the first instance, he speaks of the Samaritan as having compassion on the man (10:33b). To have compassion is to suffer with someone. Compassion is the defining statement about God that occurs in Exodus 34:6–7a: " The Lord, the Lord, the *compassionate* and gracious God, slow to anger, abounding in love and faithfulness, maintaining love to thousands and forgiving wickedness, rebellion and sin" *(New International Version).*

God's compassion and graciousness are described in the Hebrew Scriptures as the basis for God's deliverance (Psalms 40:11; 51:1; 69:16; 77:9; 79:8; 102:13); as the basis for God's remembrance of his people (2 Kings 13:23); and as the basis for God's forgiveness (Psalm 78:38; Isaiah 49:13; Micah 7:19). Compassion is also central to the restoration and reconciliation between God and his people (Hosea 2:19; Zechariah 1:16; 12:10).

This language is carried over into the behavior and ministry of Jesus, where we read he had *compassion* on the people and began to heal them (Matthew 20:34; Mark 1:41; Luke 7:13); that he had *compassion* and began to teach them (Mark 6:34); and that he had *compassion* and fed them (Matthew 15:32; Mark 8:2). In Luke, the word *compassion* occurs in only a few places: in the account of the raising of the widow's son (7:13), in this passage (10:33) and in the description of the father when he sees his prodigal son returning home (15:20). Clearly, its use in the parables of the compassionate Samaritan and the prodigal son must have had quite a strong effect in identifying the characters of the Samaritan and the father with God, which would have been totally shocking for Jesus' original hearers.

As the parable continues, Jesus describes the Samaritan as one who binds up the wounds of the man, after having poured oil and wine on them (10:34a). Again, this explicitly echoes the language used to describe God in the Hebrew Scriptures as the one who binds up the wounds of his people (Isaiah 30:26; 61:1; Jeremiah 30:17; Ezekiel 34:16; Hosea 6:1; Psalm 147:33). Likewise the use of oil and wine, while medicinally helpful in softening the traveler's wounds and cleansing them, echoes what the priest and Levite would have offered on the altar. Thus it is the Samaritan who pours out the true offering acceptable to God.

It is fair to say then that the Samaritan did for the man everything that the priest and Levite should have done, but did not. Furthermore, the Samaritan puts the man on his own donkey, takes him to an inn and pays for his immediate and continuing care, thereby explicitly countering the actions of the robbers who had robbed him and left him for dead (10:34–35).

Samaritans followed the Torah, and so the same risk of defilement from touching a dead body was present for this Samaritan as well. However, he did not allow the law to hedge him in and was compassionate to the battered man.

Jesus' question to the lawyer at the end of the story reveals how he has completely revolutionized the original question, "Who is my neighbor?" Jesus asks the lawyer: "Which of these three, do you think was a neighbor to the man who fell into the hands of the robbers?" (10:36). The lawyer replies, "The one who showed him mercy" (10:37).

Notice that the lawyer does not respond to Jesus by saying "the Samaritan." The identification of the one who showed mercy as being a Samaritan is so repulsive that the lawyer seems unable to name him. This Samaritan was not only an enemy, he was a particularly hated enemy. Any observant, pious, self-respecting Jew in a ditch would rather be left for dead than be helped by such a person.

Within this context, Jesus' question is disconcerting: "Which of these three was a neighbor?" The question suggests that mercy and compassion are what describe a neighbor. But the question also implies that the lawyer is to follow the example of his enemy, the Samaritan, in learning what it is to be a neighbor. The parable also responds to the lawyer's question, "What must I do to gain eternal life?" He must believe that God's world is a world where the most despicable enemy is discovered to be one's neighbor, capable of such unexpected goodness that those who want to relate to God must follow the actions of those they most despise.

Points for Reflection

Our very claim to be followers of Jesus places us on the list of those who should be most challenged and threatened by the parable of the compassionate Samaritan. Do we proclaim a world of such radical compassion and healing as portrayed in this parable, or do we ignore it as the priest and Levite did? Do we possibly even deny it?

The one who asks, "Who is my neighbor?" often thinks of others in the world as classifiable commodities—white Anglo-Saxon Protestant, African American, Hispanic, Southeast Asian. One can build fences to determine who is in the circle of those to be cared for and who is not. Then we can take care of "our own," thinking that our help should be directed to those we are related to by ties of family or friendship—things based on rights, bloodlines, culture, law or tradition. The example of the compassionate Samaritan, who does good to a person in need without any apparent regard for religion or ethnicity, illustrates how deep love pays no attention to religious, ethnic or cultural distinctions. The behavior of the Samaritan is the very same behavior as God's. The parable challenges all readers to examine and widen their images of God to include even the compassionate Samaritan.

Ultimately, what this parable means for us today has everything to do with how we respond to Jesus' command to the lawyer. When he says to the lawyer and to us "Go and do likewise," will we? Here is a contemporary example of someone who actively responded to Jesus' challenge, told by Richard O'Dea, a former associate dean at the University of Southern California.

A Modern Good Samaritan

Recently I was fortunate to witness a modern re-enactment of the story known as "The Good Samaritan" (Luke 10:29–37). I was giving a series of lectures on English literature at Washington State University in Pullman. Each week I would fly from Seattle, rent a car in Spokane and drive to Pullman to deliver the talk. The next day I would return to Spokane and fly back to Seattle.

After the seventh lecture, the airport in Spokane was closed because of fog, so I took the bus to Seattle. It was a milk run that infuriated my fellow passengers, businessmen who had also missed their flights. They all had meetings to make in Houston, New Orleans or New York and they voiced their frustration.

Soon after we left Spokane, the bus picked up a drunk, one of the worst I have ever seen. He looked as if he had been in a fight the night before, or perhaps had fallen through a plate-glass window, for his arms and head were covered with bloody bandages. My fellow passengers complained that he should not have been permitted to board the bus.

They had probably never in their lives seen such a person. He immediately fell asleep in the front of the bus, snoring and drooling. Then he slid halfway from his seat into the aisle, which enraged his fellow travelers even more.

At the next stop, a town named Davenport, a beautiful young woman boarded the bus. She was tall, slender, blond and elegantly dressed in a long camel's hair coat. Every masculine eye on the bus turned toward her and the complaints halted.

As we neared the Cascade Mountains, the bus became quite cold. Suddenly the young woman rose from her seat, walked up to the inebriated man, folded his arm over his chest and helped him back into his seat. Then she took off her camel's hair coat, covered him with it and returned to her seat. There was complete silence in the bus; for there was a beauty in her gesture that made us seem ugly and we all knew it.

Both the young woman and the intoxicated man left the bus in Everett, seven hours later. By then he was sober enough to hold the coat for her and thank her. Then he bent and kissed her hand. We drove off in silence, forgetting for the moment how important we thought we were.[8]

For Discussion

1. Have you ever felt forgiven by God?

2. Have you ever forgiven others or felt forgiven by others? If so, describe your feelings about that experience.

3. Do you believe that God invites you to dine with him and his friends?

4. How do excuses get in the way of your relationship with God, with loved ones, with friends?

5. Have you ever experienced the compassion of God? Describe how you act compassionately toward others.

Parables about Discipleship

"And Jesus said to them, 'Follow me and I will
make you fish for people.'"

(Mark 1:17)

Anyone who takes seriously the teachings of Jesus in
the gospels knows full well that he or she is called to be a
disciple of Jesus. This not only means emulating the life of Jesus, but
appropriating his teachings about God and fellow human beings.
The gospels provide two types of stories that deal with discipleship.
One is the parable; the other is known as the call story, in which Jesus
invites people to follow him.

Chapter Ten

Call Stories

Call stories are found in all four of the gospels. In them, Jesus calls people to follow him, that is, to appropriate his lifestyle and teachings. In the synoptic gospels we encounter the call of the first disciples (Matthew 4:18–22; Mark 1:16–20; Luke 5:1–11), the call of Levi (Matthew 9:9–13; Mark 2:13–17; Luke 5:27–32), the call of the twelve (Matthew 10:1–4; Mark 3:13–19; Luke 6:12–16), the missionary charge of the twelve (Matthew 10:17–31; Mark 6:7–13; Luke 9:1–6) and the call of the rich man (Matthew 19:16–30; Mark 17:22; Luke 18:18–30). In each of these stories, Jesus takes the initiative in calling the disciples. Each of them, with the exception of the rich man, decide to follow Jesus. This decision is what Dietrich Bonhoeffer described in his classic book, *The Cost of Discipleship*, as "an exclusive attachment to [Jesus'] person."[1] Disciples, as portrayed in the call stories, are required to leave behind their former occupations to follow Jesus. They leave the known for the unknown. These are stories of conversion and commitment. They are told by the gospel narrators as part of Jesus' public ministry and focus on the response of the disciples to Jesus' call.[2]

While the call stories deal entirely with men being called by Jesus to be disciples, it would be incorrect to conclude that Jesus did not have women followers. That Jesus had female followers as well as male followers is made clear in the gospel of Luke (see chart in chapter 5). In Luke 8:1–3, 23:49, 23:55 and 24:1–11, both named and unnamed female followers are mentioned. Female followers of Jesus are also mentioned in Acts 18:1–2. Luke and the Acts of the Apostles understand discipleship to be inclusive of men and women (see Acts 1:14).[3]

We turn our attention now to Jesus' parables about discipleship. These are stories that deal with the demands and challenges of being a disciple. They are addressed not only to Jesus' original disciples, but to all would-be disciples.

Parables on Discipleship

There are five parables that specifically deal with being a disciple of Jesus. They include the parable of the two builders (Matthew 7:24–27 and Luke 6:47–49); the conjoined parables of the tower builder and the warring king (Luke 14:28–33); the parable of the unworthy servant (Luke 17:7–10); and the parable of the laborers in the vineyard (Matthew 20:1–16).

To some extent, all of the parables of Jesus address questions of discipleship; they address the issues of how one should live in relationship to Jesus, God and others. Whether at the level of their original audience or as they apply to audiences of a subsequent age, parables are intended to provoke, to challenge and to elicit a concrete response to Jesus' invitation to discipleship. Each of the parables explored in this chapter address specific details of being a disciple of Jesus.

The Parables of the Two Builders

²⁴"Everyone then who hears these words of mine and acts on them will be like a wise man who built his house on rock. ²⁵The rain fell, the floods came, and the winds blew and beat on that house, but it did not fall, because it had been founded on rock. ²⁶And everyone who hears these words of mine and does not act on them will be like a foolish man who built his house on sand. ²⁷The rain fell, and the floods came, and the winds blew and beat against that house, and it fell—and great was its fall!" (Matthew 7:24–27)

⁴⁷I will show you what someone is like who comes to me, hears my words, and acts on them. ⁴⁸That one is like a man building a house, who dug deeply and laid the foundation on rock; when a flood arose, the river burst against that house but could not shake it, because it had been well built. ⁴⁹But the one who hears and does not act is like a man who built a house on the ground without a foundation. When the river burst against it, immediately it fell, and great was the ruin of that house." (Luke 6:47–49)

This parable is often referred to by a variety of names. It is called the parable of the house upon the rock, the parable of the two houses, the parable of the two foundations or the parable of the two builders. These are the four titles by which it is referenced in the major commentaries. Each title reveals a particular emphasis, each of which can be found in the parable. The original gospel writers did not give the parable a name.

In addition, the imagery found in this parable also appears in a second-century CE rabbinic parable. According to rabbinic tradition, Rabbi Elisha Ben Abuyah, who taught around 120 to 140 CE, spoke a parable in which he compared those who studied the Torah and did good deeds with those who studied the Torah and did not do good deeds. Concerning the first, he said this person is like someone who "builds first with stones and then with bricks," and even though a great flood of water comes and washes against the foundations, the water does not blot them out of their place. On the other hand, the second person is like someone who "builds first with bricks and then with stones," and even if only a little water comes and washes against the foundations, it immediately overturns them.[4]

The rabbinic story follows the same contours as the gospel parable, but the discussion is framed in terms of studying the Torah and doing good deeds. In the gospel parable, the discussion centers around following Jesus. However, the conclusion or the moral is the same in both, that is, action must result—from studying the Torah for the rabbis and their disciples, from heeding Jesus' interpretation of the Torah for Christians.

In both gospels, the parable closes a discourse of Jesus. In Matthew, it closes the Sermon on the Mount (Matthew 5:1—7:29). In Luke, the parable closes the

Sermon on the Plain (Luke 6:20–49). In each case, the parable's function is to move the hearers of the sermon to contemplate what has been preached and to act upon the teachings of Jesus.

Matthew's Version

Matthew envisions building a house on rock, something that is possible in many parts of Palestine. The terrain of Galilee, inland from the Mediterranean Sea to Upper Galilee in the north and the Sea of Galilee in the east, includes hilly and mountainous areas of sandstone, basalt, rock and limestone. In addition, portions of Judea around Jerusalem have a limestone base. The Temple at Jerusalem stood securely on a rock base (Isaiah 28:16). Rock is also a metaphor for a solid, stable foundation (Psalm 40:2; Sirach 40:15), and frequently God is pictured as the rock on which one can be secure (1 Samuel 2:2; Psalm 18:2, 32; Psalm 31:2–3; Psalm 71:3).

Furthermore, the parable's language of "building on a rock" (7:24) anticipates Peter's commissioning in Matthew 16:18: "On this rock I will build my church." In both passages the teaching is much the same, that is, even the greatest affliction—"the gates of Haides [Hell]" will not prevail (16:18). For Matthew, the point is not simply that Jesus and the obedient follower each build on solid foundations. Matthew has in mind the traditional Jewish concept of the Temple as having been founded on a rock that stands at the gateway to both heaven and the underworld. Thus, in the context of both Jesus' ministry and teachings, the parable of the two builders conveys a challenge to "build a house" on a foundation equivalent to that on which God's own house is set.

Probably more to the point, since Matthew and Luke both wrote after the fall of Jerusalem and its Temple—"the city and house of God"—to the Romans in 70 CE, they attest to the fact that "the ruin of that house was great" (Luke 6:49). The historical context of the evangelists' own day suggests that those who acted or failed to act on Jesus' words would have already faced a crisis that only those with firm foundations would withstand.

Furthermore, it is likely that the "house" referred to in the parable is the church, whose foundation is Jesus. Thus the torrential weather that the church will have to endure will not tear it loose from its secure foundation that is the Lord.

Matthew cites three elements of bad weather in his version of the parable: heavy rain, unexpected flash floods and extreme winds. These elements can befall inhabitants of Palestine during the rainy season (October to April). When rain falls in significant amounts, it comes down from the mountains and hills of the upper regions. It fills wadis quickly and creates streams where none existed before. The person who both listens to Jesus and appropriates his lifestyle can easily weather these elements. The community of disciples known as the church can also weather these elements.

Matthew's version creatively contrasts the wisdom of the house builder who builds on rock with the folly of the person who builds on sand. True wisdom for Matthew comes in accepting Jesus, the rock whom the builders rejected as both the cornerstone (Matthew 21:42) and foundation for both the church and anyone building his or her house of faith and practice of discipleship. This was marvelously affirmed in the opening line of the hymn: "The church's one foundation is Jesus Christ her Lord."[5]

Luke's Version

In Luke, the builder who builds on rock exercises great care in the building process. Three activities are mentioned in the original Greek of the text: He dug, he went down deep and he laid a foundation. The words of the NRSV ("who dug deeply and laid the foundation") do not capture the full sense of how hard he worked. Luke's point, of course, is that true discipleship requires hard work, as hard as manual labor. Furthermore, in Luke the house built on rock, which is a metaphor for the church, not only stands firm, it is not even shaken. The house is sturdy because it is well-built as a result of the extensive labor.

The disciple who hears and does the teachings of Jesus is compared to such a builder. That disciple is well prepared for the "rush of mighty waters" in a "time of distress" (Psalm 32:6) and can be considered sound. His or her faith and commitment is rock solid.

Luke's version of the parable mentions only a flood. The Greek term used is of a river overflowing its banks. Since Luke's audience does not dwell in Palestine, a flood with a river as its source may make more sense. But the flood also has theological meaning. It harkens back to the flood story and Noah (Genesis 6—9). Just as Noah was faithful to God and was not destroyed by the flood, so the faithful disciple of Jesus will not be swept away by the floodwaters of chaos. Just as Noah heard, listened and acted on what God asked of him, the disciple is to listen and act on what Jesus asks of him or her.

Points for Reflection

People who have volunteered to help build a house for Habitat for Humanity know how important the foundation of the house is. It is the first item constructed, and the person who supervises the building of the foundation has to be listened to for the house to be sturdy. The same is true in the parable of the two builders. Those who listen to Jesus will not only build a good house of faith (a church), but their faith as disciples will not be shaken.

The parable forces the reader of every generation to realize that discipleship includes obedience to Jesus. A disciple must listen to the words he speaks in the Sermons on the Mount and on the Plain, but these words must lead to the actions that he demands. These include practicing the beatitudes, praying, not hiding one's light—one's time, talent and treasure.

The parable of the two builders requires one to reflect on true wisdom. The wise builder digs deep and lays his or her foundation for life on the word of God (both the sacred scriptures and Jesus). At times, this requires one to keep digging until you get in touch with the rock-solid revelation of God in the person of Jesus, and then building your life upon that rock.

How do you put your life together after a storm? Many have found that faith in God is the only thing that gives them the strength to keep going, renew their hope and make a new beginning. We do not choose whether we will face storms in life—they just come along. Yet faith is the firm foundation we are called to stand on as disciples of Jesus who weather life's storms.

The real mystery of discipleship is that it is as much listening and receiving as it is doing and striving. The simple call of Jesus to follow him always means a radical change of life.

Parables of the Tower Builder and Warring King

²⁸For which of you, intending to build a tower, does not first sit down and estimate the cost, to see whether he has enough to complete it? ²⁹Otherwise, when he has laid a foundation and is not able to finish, all who see it will begin to ridicule him, ³⁰saying, 'This fellow began to build and was not able to finish.' ³¹Or what king, going out to wage war against another king, will not sit down first and consider whether he is able with ten thousand to oppose the one who comes against him with twenty thousand? ³²If he cannot, then, while the other is still far away, he sends a delegation and asks for the terms of peace. ³³So therefore, none of you can become my disciple if you do not give up all your possessions. (Luke 14:28–33)

From the building of houses we turn to the building of a tower and the strategy for waging war. These two parables begin with a challenge to the hearers: "Who among you?" In the gospels, Jesus is often depicted as using this rhetorical device to require assent. For example, he asks: "Who among you would not rescue your livestock on the Sabbath?" (paraphrasing Matthew 12:11). The answer is obvious, so he concludes: "How much more valuable is a human being than a sheep! So it is lawful to do good on the Sabbath" (Matthew 12:12). The question, "Who among you?" is intended to elicit agreement from the hearer. It is an appeal to logic not often used in the parables, yet it is profoundly thought-provoking.

The context of these two parables in Luke's gospel allows for little ambiguity regarding either their meaning or their intended audience. Large crowds were accompanying Jesus. Possibly fearing that they had failed to grasp the radical nature of God's reign—God's breaking into their lives—or its drastic implications for discipleship, Jesus issues a blunt challenge: Whoever does not hate the members of his or her family "cannot be my disciple," and whoever does not take up his own cross—whoever is not prepared to die—"cannot be my disciple" (Luke 14:25–27). The parables that follow illustrate his point.

In the first, someone sets out to build a tower.⁶ Will that person not determine in advance whether he possesses sufficient resources to complete the task successfully? If he doesn't, the would-be builder will reap the mockery and scorn of the

136

onlookers. In the second, a king contemplates the cost of going to war, weighing the chances of a successful campaign and possible victory against an opponent who commands an army twice the size of his own. If his forces are insufficient, will he not then be forced to negotiate either a surrender or a peace treaty?

It is not at all difficult to see these paired parables and their characters as two different aspects of discipleship. In the first, Jesus says, "Decide whether you can afford to follow me." In the second, he says, "Decide whether you can afford to refuse my demands." Yet any differences in emphasis between the two parables appear to be overpowered by the force of Jesus' concluding exhortation: "So therefore none of you can become my disciple if you do not give up all of your possessions" (Luke 14:33).

The renunciation of all of one's possessions is consistent with Luke's emphasis on the demands of discipleship. In Luke's gospel Jesus seeks to dissuade his listeners from too easy a view of discipleship. That possessions can pose an obstacle to discipleship is a constantly recurring theme in Luke's gospel. Jesus warns: "Take care! Be on your guard against all kinds of greed; for one's life does not consist in the abundance of possessions" (12:15). Jesus counsels: "Sell your possessions and give alms" (12:33). The fishermen called to be disciples leave everything behind to follow Jesus (5:11), as does Levi (5:28). Zaccheus is exemplary for giving half of his possessions to the poor (19:8). The Galilean women use their financial resources to support the mission of Jesus (8:3). Letting go of the vice grip of possessions has as its aim to both free the heart from being centered on them (12:34) and to ensure that there are none in need (Acts 4:34).

The two parables conclude that following Jesus or refusing to follow him cost one's all. It is not a question of risk management; it is a question of commitment. Will one lose all as a follower of Jesus and for the sake of God's reign, or will one refuse to follow? In other words, which is the more promising course of action?

Points for Reflection

The parables of the tower builder and warring king are simple and straightforward, but the teachings on discipleship that surround them are possibly the most radical in the gospel of Luke. The parables are preceded by Jesus' challenge: "Whoever does not carry the cross and follow me cannot be my disciple" (Luke 14:27). Furthermore, the parables are followed by yet another challenge from the lips of Jesus: "None of you can become my disciple if you do not give up all your possessions" (Luke 14:33).

The language of cross-bearing is often misunderstood, especially by Americans. Bearing a cross has nothing to do with enduring chronic illness, difficult family conditions or relationships or even painful physical conditions. It is instead what we do voluntarily as a consequence of our commitment to Jesus Christ. Cross-bearing requires deliberate sacrifice and exposure to risk and ridicule in order to follow Jesus. This commitment is not just a way of life, however. It is a commitment to a person—to Jesus. A disciple follows another person and learns a new way of life. The crucified Jesus can be no stranger to a disciple.

In a sense, no one can know whether he or she will be able to fulfill a commitment to discipleship. But Jesus was not asking for a guarantee of complete fidelity in advance. If he had, no one would qualify to be a disciple. Through these parables, Jesus was simply calling for each person who would be a disciple to consider in advance what the commitment requires, what the job description includes.

The cost of discipleship is paid in many different kinds of currency. For some people, a redirection of time and energy away from self and toward others is required; for others, a change of personal relationships, a change in vocation or a new attitude toward personal possessions is needed. But for each person, the call to discipleship is an all-consuming call to conversion. A complete change of priorities is required of all would-be disciples. No part-time disciples are needed. No partial commitments are accepted.

The Parable of the Unworthy Servant

7"Who among you would say to your slave who has just come in from plowing or tending sheep in the field, 'Come here at once and take your place at the table'? 8Would you not rather say to him, 'Prepare supper for me, put on your apron and serve me while I eat and drink; later you may eat and drink'? 9Do you thank the slave for doing what was commanded? 10So you also, when you have done all that you were ordered to do, say, 'We are worthless slaves; we have done only what we ought to have done!'" (Luke 17:7–10)

This parable bears several key resemblances to the parables of the tower builder and the warring king. It, too, is found only in Luke; it challenges the listener/reader. "Who among you . . ." it is addressed to disciples (17:1–5), and it proclaims the conditions of discipleship in a clearly uncompromising manner.

The Greek noun for the main character in the parable is *doulos* and can be translated as either "slave" or "servant." In the time of the gospel, no servant can expect to serve his or her own needs first. Rather, it is the essence of servanthood to place the requirements of one's master above one's own need, no matter how inconvenient doing so may be. The same, Jesus says, is true of discipleship.

The literary genius of the parable rests in its adoption of different perspectives on the situation to make its point. The first three verses (7–9) assume the perspective of the master or, stated more precisely, they invite the listener to assume such a perspective.

It is part of the servant's job description to prepare and to serve his master's main meal. The master is in no way indebted to the servant for having completed this daily chore. Does the master owe the servant anything? Of course not! Any right-minded first-century listener would be expected to agree that servants simply serve and that there would be no point in anyone thinking otherwise.

Having won over the agreement from the listeners, Jesus springs the rhetorical trap. No longer assuming the perspective of the master, but addressing the audience as servants or slaves, Jesus says, "So you also when you have done all that you were ordered to do, say, 'We are worthless slaves; we have done only what we ought to have done!'" (Luke 17:10). If they agree from the perspective of the master, how much more must Jesus' hearers agree if they are really only servants. And thus if such service and submission are required of human relationships, how much more are they required in our relations with God and in our obedience to all that God commands?

Taken by itself, the first half of the parable denies the follower any role in setting the terms of discipleship. And the second half denies the possibility that service for God is intrinsically meritorious. This admonition is addressed to Jesus' disciples in every era.

In Jesus' day, the role of a disciple was not simply to learn, but also to act as a servant. A disciple's service required performing a variety of essential, yet menial, tasks for the teacher. Thus, two of Jesus' disciples fetch a donkey for him to ride (Luke 19:29–35), and Peter and John prepare the Passover meal (Luke 22:8–13).

Yet Jesus' disciples are portrayed as sometimes thinking that their association with their master allows some special status or somehow gives them special benefits. For example, they are presented as attempting to keep a non-disciple from using Jesus' name (Luke 9:49), seeking special favors from Jesus (Mark 10:35–37) and arguing among themselves as to which of them was the greatest (Luke 22:24). Insofar as the disciples act as servants to Jesus, the intent of the parable of the unworthy servant is to point out that such service does not constitute a claim on Jesus' favor, much less a claim on God's favor. Finally, the parable provides a creative ambiguity as to the identity of the master of the slave or servant, who may be God, as Jewish piety of the day would have interpreted it, or who might be Jesus, as the disciples would expect. Or perhaps both.

Points for Reflection

This parable is probably no one's favorite, yet it forces us to reexamine our assumptions about our relationship with God. The major difficulty is that while the parable makes a significant point about discipleship and humility before God, it presents God in the unappealing role of a slave driver. While such an image might be appropriate in the first century, most of us would probably choose a completely different metaphor. Our normal inclination is that if we do what we are commanded, we deserve some reward.

Regardless, God owes us nothing for living good Christian lives. God's presence, favor and blessing are matters of pure grace. They are a gift; they cannot be earned.[7] As disciples, we may never assume that we can deal with God on the basis of what God owes us. To do so is to have rejected the gift of grace as the basis of our relationship with God and to base that relationship on our own worth and merit. Grace, by definition, is a gift, freely given by God, freely accepted (not merited) by us.

The Laborers and the Vineyard

[1]"For the kingdom of heaven is like a landowner who went out early in the morning to hire laborers for his vineyard. [2]After agreeing with the laborers for the usual daily wage, he sent them into his vineyard. [3]When he went out about nine o'clock, he saw others standing idle in the marketplace; [4]and he said to them, 'You also go into the vineyard, and I will pay you whatever is right.' So they went. [5]When he went out again about noon and about three o'clock, he did the same. [6]And about five o'clock he went out and found others standing around; and he said to them, 'Why are you standing here idle all day?' [7]They said to him, 'Because no one has hired us.' He said to them, 'You also go into the vineyard.' [8]When evening came, the owner of the vineyard said to his manager, 'Call the laborers and give them their pay, beginning with the last and then going to the first.' [9]When those hired about five o'clock came, each of them received the usual daily wage. [10]Now when the first came, they thought they would receive more; but each of them also received the usual daily wage. [11]And when they received it, they grumbled against the landowner, [12]saying, 'These last worked only one hour, and you have made them equal to us who have borne the burden of the day and the scorching heat.' [13]But he replied to one of them, 'Friend, I am doing you no wrong; did you not agree with me for the usual daily wage? [14]Take what belongs to you and go; I choose to give to this last the same as I give to you. [15]Am I not allowed to do what I choose with what belongs to me? Or are you envious because I am generous?' [16]So the last will be first, and the first will be last." (Matthew 20:1–16)

From parables unique to Luke we turn to a parable unique to Matthew that deals with discipleship. In the parable of the laborers in the vineyard, workers hired at different hours represent disciples and the landowner represents God. The workers in the parable expect to be compensated proportionately; much to their astonishment, however, they all receive the same wage.

This parable has been interpreted in a variety of ways by such great church fathers as Irenaeus (c. 130–200 CE), Origen of Alexandria (c. 184–254 CE) and John Chrysostom (c. 347–407 CE). No attempt will be made here to delineate each of their interpretations, except to say that each one centers around the different times that the workers are called to labor in the vineyard, which is a stock metaphor for Israel (Isaiah 5:1–7; Jeremiah 12:10).

This parable begins in the familiar world in which day laborers are hired at sunup and are paid at the end of the day in accordance with Torah regulation and Jewish practice (Leviticus 19:13; Deuteronomy 24:14–15). A dinarius was a normal day's pay for a manual laborer hired for the day, but barely enough to maintain a family at the subsistence level. The first-century reader feels at home in the world created by the story.

The parable gradually fades into another dimension from that of the every-day world, as unusual features begin to accumulate for which no explanation is given. Instead of sending his manager, the wealthy landowner himself goes to the market to hire laborers (20:1–7). The landowner goes repeatedly, even at the "eleventh hour" (5:00 PM). No explanation is given as to why those "standing idle" had not been hired on earlier recruitment visits. The first group of workers is hired on the basis of an oral contract for the normal amount; the later groups are promised "whatever is right," thus raising, but not answering, the question of what is "right." Although the first group has a "contract" while the second can only trust in the master's sense of justice, in reality both groups depend on the trustworthiness of the landowner. In the closing scene, in which all are paid the same, the middle groups are ignored in order to focus on "first" and "last."

The closing scene, in which payment is made, contains the deeply disturbing element that makes the story a parable rather than the illustration of a logical point. At the landowner's order, those hired last are paid first. They receive a full day's pay. Those hired first now expect to receive more (verse 10), but they receive the agreed-upon amount. Matthew's readers who assume they are committed to justice—equal pay for equal work—share the consternation of those who have worked all day, enduring its heat and fatigue.

The parable is upsetting because it functions to challenge and to reverse conventional values, including the sense of justice and fairness among Matthew's religious readership. This is one reason why Matthew chose to preserve it and insert it here. Here, as elsewhere, Matthew understands the parable allegorically. For him, the landowner is the eschatological judge, God or Jesus, who is indeed "good," and the payment at the end of the day (the twelfth hour) is the last judgment. The "first" and "last" in Matthew's view both refer to insiders, to Christians who have worked long and faithfully and to latecomers who have not. Some members of Matthew's church might have read "first" as the old-line Jewish Christians and "last" as Gentile Christians, both of whom are now received on an equal basis.

The parable deals with resentment toward others who have actually received the grace one affirms in theory. A careful comparison of verses 10 and 12 is instructive. Those who had worked all day begin *not* by objecting to the grace others had received, but by expecting that they themselves will receive more (verse 10). When they receive the just fulfillment of their contract, they object *not* to what they have in fact received, but that others have been made equal to them. They have what they have by justice; others have been made equal by grace. It is this last resentment that they find unbearable. Their objection to God's gracious acceptance of others as their equals alienates them.

The parable invites reflection on the sovereignty of the good God, the one with whom there can be no bargaining because he is the creator and the sovereign.[8] Likewise, the parable, while affirming the sovereign grace of God, addresses the issue of discipleship.

The moral of the story is that "the last will be first and the first last" (verse 16). This has led to suggestions that the parable refers to Jews and Gentiles or, perhaps, to Christians of Jewish and Gentile origins, respectively. Or, if interpreted strictly within Israel, perhaps it should be seen as referring to scribes and Pharisees, on the one hand, in comparison to sinners and outcasts on the other.

Yet the proverb about the "first" and the "last" in Matthew's gospel can be equally applied to disciples who have abandoned everything to follow Jesus. It suggests that those who have nothing with which to commend themselves can still look forward to a rich compensation in the reign of God. And if this is the meaning of the parable as well, then the disciples are portrayed as those who have been hired last in the day and rewarded more on the basis of God's generosity than on the basis of their own accomplishments.

Points for Reflection

As with so many parables, the situation at first seems ludicrous. From a strictly human vantage point, it does not seem fair. Why should those who worked only a couple of hours get the same wage as those who bore the heat of the day? But then, the reign of God does not operate on our human principles of justice. The teaching revolves around the reversal of first and last and the fact that what is most important is not *when* one chooses to answer Jesus' call to discipleship, but *if* one chooses to follow Jesus at all. The positioning of the images of first and last call attention to God's incredible generosity toward all who work in the vineyard (19:30; 20:8, 16). Being a member of God's realm is not a reward for work accomplished, but a gift freely given by God. The challenge to disciples of every age is to be gracious receivers of God's gift.

For Discussion

1. Do you feel you have been called to be a disciple of Jesus?

2. What is the foundation upon which your faith is built?

3. How do you take up your cross and follow Jesus?

4. If God's grace cannot be merited, why seek it?

5. How do you react to God offering the same gift to those who have served a short time as disciples as well as to those who have served a long time as disciples?

Appendix

The Parables of Jesus in the Lectionary

One of the better-known results of the reforms of the Second Vatican Council (1962–1965) was the renewed emphasis on the place of the Bible within Catholic life, as well as greater attention to its use in worship, study and devotion. For most Catholics, their main exposure to the Bible occurs when they assemble to celebrate the eucharist.

With this in mind, the bishops of the church assembled at the council called for reforms and changes in how sacred scripture was to be used at liturgy. In poetic fashion, they said, "The treasures of the Bible are to be opened up more lavishly, so that richer fare may be provided for the faithful at the table of God's word" (*Constitution on the Sacred Liturgy*, 51). To that end, they provided for a redesign of the lectionary, which is the book that contains the assigned readings for Sunday and daily eucharist as well as the major feasts of the church. It is arranged according to the liturgical seasons of Advent, Christmas, Lent, Triduum, Easter and Ordinary Time.

The planners of the Sunday lectionary decided on a three-year cycle. One of the three synoptic gospels forms the central focus of each of the Sundays of each year in Ordinary Time. In Year A, the gospel of Matthew is the primary gospel that is read; in Year B, it is the gospel of Mark; and in Year C, it is the gospel of Luke. The gospel of John is not neglected, however. In accord with ancient tradition of the church, John has always been read during the Lent and Easter seasons. In addition, because of the shortness of the gospel of Mark, chapter 6 of John (the bread of life discourse) is taken up on five Sundays during Year B.

This particular arrangement of the lectionary allows Catholics to hear each of the gospels in its own right, over the course of a year. This enables Catholics to come to know the distinctive picture of Jesus and his teachings presented by Matthew, Mark and Luke, respectively.

Turning our attention now to the parables and the three-year cycle of Sunday gospel readings, we discover that on twelve Sundays in Year A, parables from the gospel of Matthew are to be read, and the same twelve appear on various weekdays. In addition, four other parables of Matthew are read on weekdays. In Year B, five parables from the gospel of Mark are assigned for reading on Sunday. Of these five, four are also assigned to weekdays. In addition, three other parables of Mark are assigned for weekdays. In Year C, seventeen parables of the gospel of Luke are assigned to be read on Sundays, and all but one of these is repeated in the weekday lectionary. The parable of the prodigal son, which is found only in the gospel of Luke, is read on two Sundays. In addition, eight parables of the gospel of Luke that do not appear in the Sunday lectionary are assigned as a weekday reading. Finally, Luke's version of the parable of the vineyard and tenants (20:9–19) is omitted from use in the lectionary.

What follows is a listing of the parables from the synoptic gospels that are assigned for reading in the lectionary for Sundays and weekdays. The list is provided to help readers see how integral the parables are to the celebration of the eucharistic liturgy of the church.

Parables from the Gospel of Matthew

Matthew 5:13–16 Fifth Sunday in Ordinary Time, A

Tuesday, Tenth Week in Ordinary Time

Matthew 7:21–27 Ninth Sunday in Ordinary Time, A

Thursday, First Week of Advent (Matthew 7:21, 24–27)

Thursday, Twelfth Week in Ordinary Time (Matthew 7:21–29)

Matthew 9:14–17 Saturday, Thirteenth Week in Ordinary Time

Matthew 13:1–23 Fifteenth Sunday in Ordinary Time, A

Wednesday, Sixteenth Week in Ordinary Time (Matthew 13:1–9)

Thursday, Sixteenth Week Ordinary Time (Matthew 13:10–17)

Friday, Sixteenth Week in Ordinary Time (Matthew 13:18–23)

Matthew 13:24–43 Sixteenth Sunday in Ordinary Time, A

Saturday, Sixteenth Week in Ordinary Time (Matthew 13:24–30)

Monday, Seventeenth Week in Ordinary Time (Matthew 13:31–35)

Tuesday, Seventeenth Week in Ordinary Time (Matthew 13:36–43)

Matthew 13:44–52 Seventeenth Sunday in Ordinary Time, A

Wednesday, Seventeenth Week in Ordinary Time (Matthew 13:44–46)

Thursday, Seventeenth Week in Ordinary Time (Matthew 13:47–53)

Matthew 15:1–2, 10–14 Tuesday, Eighteenth Week in Ordinary Time

Matthew 18:12–14 Tuesday, Nineteenth Week in Ordinary Time

144

Matthew 18:21–35	Twenty-fourth Sunday in Ordinary Time, A
	Tuesday, Third Week of Lent
	Thursday, Nineteenth Week in Ordinary Time (Matthew 18:21—19:1)
Matthew 20:1–16a	Twenty-fifth Sunday in Ordinary Time, A
	Wednesday, Twentieth Week in Ordinary Time
Matthew 21:28–32	Twenty-sixth Sunday in Ordinary Time, A
	Tuesday, Third Week of Lent
Matthew 21:33–43	Twenty-seventh Sunday in Ordinary Time
	Friday, Second Week of Lent (Matthew 21:33–43, 45–46)
Matthew 22:1–14	Twenty-eighth Sunday in Ordinary Time, A
	Thursday, Twentieth Week in Ordinary Time
Matthew 24:45–51	Thursday, Twenty-first Week in Ordinary Time
Matthew 25:1–13	Thirty-second Sunday in Ordinary Time, A
	Friday, Twenty-first Week in Ordinary Time
Matthew 25:14–30	Thirty-third Sunday in Ordinary Time, A
	Saturday, Twenty-first Week in Ordinary Time

Parables from the Gospel of Mark

Mark 2:18–22	Eighth Sunday in Ordinary Time, B
	Monday, Second Week in Ordinary Time
Mark 3:20–35	Tenth Sunday in Ordinary Time, B
	Monday, Third Week in Ordinary Time (Mark 3:22–30)
Mark 4:1–20	Wednesday, Third Week in Ordinary Time
Mark 4:21–25	Thursday, Third Week in Ordinary Time
Mark 4:26–34	Eleventh Sunday in Ordinary Time, B
	Friday, Third Week in Ordinary Time

Mark 7:1–8,	Twenty-second Sunday in Ordinary Time, B
14–15, 21–23	Wednesday, Fifth Week in Ordinary Time (Mark 7:14–23)
Mark 12:1–12	Monday, Ninth Week in Ordinary Time
Mark 13:24–32	Thirty-third Sunday in Ordinary Time, B

Parables from the Gospel of Luke

Luke 13:1–9	Third Sunday of Lent, C
	Saturday, Twenty-ninth Week in Ordinary Time
Luke 15:1–3, 11–32	Fourth Sunday of Lent, C
	Saturday, Second Week of Lent
Luke 4:21–30	Fourth Sunday in Ordinary Time, A
	Monday, Twenty-second Week in Ordinary Time (Luke 4:16–30)
Luke 5:33–39	Friday, Twenty-second Week in Ordinary Time
Luke 6:39–45	Eighth Sunday in Ordinary Time, C
	Friday, Twenty-third Week in Ordinary Time (Luke 6:39–42)
Luke 6:43–49	Saturday, Twenty-third Week in Ordinary Time
Luke 7:31–35	Wednesday, Twenty-fourth Week in Ordinary Time
Luke 7:36–8:3	Eleventh Sunday in Ordinary Time, C
	Thursday, Twenty-fourth Week in Ordinary Time (Luke 7:36–50)
Luke 8:4–15	Saturday, Twenty-fourth Week in Ordinary Time
Luke 10:25–37	Fifteenth Sunday in Ordinary Time, C
	Monday, Twenty-seventh Week in Ordinary Time
Luke 11:1–13	Seventeenth Sunday in Ordinary Time, C
	Thursday, Twenty-seventh Week in Ordinary Time

Luke 12:13–21	Eighteenth Sunday in Ordinary Time, C
	Monday, Twenty-ninth Week in Ordinary Time
Luke 12:32–48	Nineteenth Sunday in Ordinary Time, C
	Tuesday, Twenty-ninth Week in Ordinary Time (Luke 12:35–38)
	Wednesday, Twenty-ninth Week in Ordinary Time (Luke 12:39–48)
Luke 13:18–21	Tuesday, Thirtieth Week in Ordinary Time
Luke 14:1, 7–14	Twenty-second Sunday in Ordinary Time, C
	Saturday, Thirtieth Week in Ordinary Time (Luke 14:1, 7–11)
Luke 14:15–24	Tuesday, Thirty-first Week in Ordinary Time
Luke 14:25–33	Twenty-third Sunday in Ordinary Time, C
	Wednesday, Thirty-first Week in Ordinary Time
Luke 15:1–32	Twenty-fourth Sunday in Ordinary Time, C
	Feast of the Sacred Heart of Jesus (Luke 15:3–7)
	Thursday, Thirty-first Week in Ordinary Time (Luke 15:1–10)
Luke 16:1–13	Twenty-fifth Sunday in Ordinary Time, C
	Friday, Thirty-first Week in Ordinary Time (Luke 16:1–8)
Luke 16:19–31	Twenty-sixth Sunday in Ordinary Time, C
	Thursday, Second Week of Lent
Luke 17:5–10	Twenty-seventh Sunday in Ordinary Time, C
	Tuesday, Thirty-second Week in Ordinary Time (Luke 17:7–10)
Luke 18:1–8	Twenty-ninth Sunday in Ordinary Time, C
	Saturday, Thirty-second Week in Ordinary Time
Luke 18:9–14	Thirtieth Sunday in Ordinary Time, C
Luke 19:11–28	Wednesday, Thirty-third Week in Ordinary Time
Luke 21:29–33	Friday, Thirty-fourth Week in Ordinary Time

Endnotes

Chapter One

1 John Shea, *Stories of God* (Chicago: Thomas More Press, 1978), 126.

2 Dietrich Bonhoeffer, *The Cost of Discipleship* (London: SCM Press, 1959), 49.

3 Carlo M. Martini, *The Spiritual Journey of the Apostles* (Boston: St. Paul Books & Media, 1991), 39.

4 John Shea, *Stories of God* (Chicago: Thomas More Press, 1978), 8.

5 Monika K. Hellwig, *Jesus the Compassion of God* (Wilmington, Delaware: Michael Glazier, 1983), 121.

Chapter Two

1 Andy Frankel, "A Sacred Pilgrimage: Stories of the Spirit" in the *National Storytelling Directory* (Storytelling Foundation International, 1996), 118.

2 As quoted in John Shea, *Stories of God* (Chicago: Thomas More Press, 1978), 67.

3 Michael Shermis and Arthur E. Zannoni, eds., *Introduction to Jewish Christian Relations* (Mahwah, N.J.: Paulist Press, 1991), 7–8.

4 It is becoming more common today, as we pursue of serious interfaith dialogue, to refer to the Bible in the terms "Hebrew Scriptures" and "Christian Scriptures" rather than "Old Testament" and "New Testament." Many feel that the use of the terms *old* and *new* is insulting to our Jewish brothers and sisters, whose sacred writings are not old to them in the sense of being outdated, outmoded or surpassed in value by later writings. Therefore, out of respect for our Jewish friends, our ancestors in faith, we will refer in this book to the Hebrew and Christian Scriptures rather than the Old and New Testaments.

5 The Hebrew Scriptures contains approximately ten parables that loosely resemble those of Jesus. See: Judges 9:8–15; 2 Samuel 12:1–4; 14:4–7; 1 Kings 20:38–43; 2 Kings 14:8–10; Isaiah 5:1–7; Ezekiel 17:2–10; 19:1–9; 19:10–14; 21:1–5; 24:2–5. For further reading, see T. W. Manson, *The Teachings of Jesus: Studies of Its Form and Content* (Cambridge: Cambridge University Press, 1948), 59–66.

6 Before the development of ecumenical and interreligious dialogue, Christians dated everything BC ("Before Christ") or AD (*Anno Domini*, "in the year of our Lord"). Our newly acquired sensitivity fosters the use of BCE ("Before the Common Era") instead of BC, and CE ("Common Era") instead of AD The term *Common Era* refers to the era Jews and Christians share in common.

7 Thomas Clemens and Michael Wyschogrod, eds., *Parable and Story in Judaism and Christianity* (Mahwah, NJ: Paulist Press, 1989), 27.

8 *The New Interpreter's Bible* (Volume 9). (Nashville: Abingdon Press, 1995), 297.

9 Elie Wiesel, *The Gates of the Forest.* (New York: Holt, Rinehart and Winston, 1966), i–iii.

10 Megan McKenna, *Parables: The Arrows of God* (Maryknoll, N.Y.: Orbis, 1994), 63.

11 For a nuanced interpretation along the lines of its image for God, see Arthur E. Zannoni, *Tell Me Your Name: Images of God in the Bible* (Chicago: Liturgy Training Publications, 2000), 57–67.

12 John Shea, *Gospel Light* (New York: Crossroad, 1998), 177.

Chapter Three

1 The complex issues surrounding the origin of the gospel of Mark are addressed in *The Literary Guide to the Bible* (Cambridge, Mass: Harvard University Press, 1987). Further explanation about the origin of the gospel of Mark is narrated in Raymond E. Brown, *An Introduction to the New Testament* (New York: Doubleday, 1997), 126-70.

2 For the various Jewish customs and Aramaic expressions found in the gospel of Mark, see Mark 3:17; 5:41; 7:3-4; 7:11; 7:34; 15:22, 15:34.

3 James Hoover, *Mark: Follow Me* (Downers Grove, Ill: InterVarsity, 1985), 8.

4 John Shea, *Gospel Light* (New York: Crossroad Publishing Co., 1998), 127-128.

Chapter Four

1 For a detailed description of this theory, see the entry "Matthew" in *Harper's Bible Commentary,* James L. Mays, general editor (San Francisco: Harper & Row Publishers, 1988), 951ff.

2 For detailed explanations of the parables in Matthew chapter 13, see either Ivor H. Hones, *The Matthean Parables: A Literary & Historical Commentary* (Leiden: Brill, 1995) or Jack D. Kingsbury, The Parables of Jesus in Matthew 13 (St. Louis: Clayton, 1969).

3 See W.D. Davies and Dale C. Allison, *A Critical and Exegetical Commentary on the Gospel According to St. Matthew,* vol. 2 (Edinburgh: T&T Clark, 1991).

4 See J. Lambrecht, *Out of the Treasure: The Parables In the Gospel of Matthew* (Louvain: Peeters; Grand Rapids: Eerdmans, 1992).

5 Arthur E. Zannoni, *Tell Me Your Name: Images of God In the Bible* (Chicago: Liturgy Training Publications, 2000) 67–68.

6 *Op cit.,* Lambrecht, p. 96.

7 John R. Donohue, *The Gospel in Parable* (Minneapolis: Fortress Press, 1988), 95–96.

Chapter Five

1 For a more thorough and detailed background information on the gospel of Luke, see Raymond E. Brown, *Introduction to the New Testament* (New York: Doubleday, 1997), 225–278.

2 For an in-depth analysis of women in the New Testament and specifically in the gospel of Luke, see Bonnie Thurston, *Women in the New Testament* (New York: The

Crossroad Publishing Co., 1998), 96–128. See also Barbara E. Reid, *Choosing the Better Part? Women in the Gospel of Luke* (Collegeville: The Liturgical Press, 1996).

3 For the treatment of the Holy Spirit in Luke, see Arthur E. Zannoni, *Tell Me Your Name: Images of God in the Bible* (Chicago: Liturgy Training Publications, 2000), 81–82.

4 The text of the ten meal stories in Luke are as follows: 5:27–39; 7:36–50; 9:10–17; 10:38–42; 11:37–54; 14:1–24; 19:1–10; 22:14–38; 24:13–35; 24:36–53. For a detailed commentary, see Eugene LaVerdiere, *Dining in the Kingdom of God* (Chicago: Liturgy Training Publications, 1994).

5 The Muratorian Fragment is contained in English translation in E. Hennecke and W. Schneemelcher, *New Testament Apocrypha* (London: 1963–65), vol. 1, pages 42–45.

6 For a detailed argument on Luke being a Gentile, see Raymond E. Brown, *Introduction to the New Testament* (New York: Doubleday, 1997), 268. For a detailed discussion of the identity of the evangelist Luke, see Joseph A. Fitzmyer, *The Gospel According to Luke* (Anchor Bible, vol. 28; Garden City, NY: Doubleday, 1981), 35–53.

7 No parable is given a title in the Greek text of the gospel of Luke. However, modern English translations of the Bible often do provide titles. For example, Luke 8:4–15 is titled by the *New American Bible and the New Jerusalem Bible* as the "Parable of the Sower," whereas in the 1970 edition of the *New American Bible* it is called the "Parable of the Seed." *The Revised English Bible* simply titles chapter 8 of Luke as "Parables." The *New Revised Standard Version* does not title the parable, thus allowing for various interpretations.

8 For a more detailed explanation and further references, see T.W. Manson, *The Teaching of Jesus* (Cambridge: Cambridge University Press, 1951), 133.

9 For further suggestions surrounding the image of the kingdom of God, see Arthur E. Zannoni, *Jesus of the Gospels: Teacher, Storyteller, Friend, Messiah* (Cincinnati: St. Anthony Messenger Press, 1996), 55–64. Further interpretations of the kingdom are found in Bruce Chilton, *The Kingdom of God* (Philadelphia: Fortress Press, 1984) and in Norman Perrin, *Jesus and the Language of the Kingdom* (Philadelphia: Fortress Press, 1976).

10 See Bernard Brandon Scott, *Hear Then the Parables* (Minneapolis: Fortress, 1989), 324–25.

11 For further reading on God imaged as a woman, see the excellent treatment of Elizabeth Johnson, *She Who Is* (New York: Crossroad, 1992).

Chapter Six

1 John Drury, *The Parables of Jesus: History and Allegory* (London: SPCK; New York: Crossroad, 1985), 139.

2 For a detailed explanation of the Pharisee understanding of purity and impurity, see Jacob Neusner, "Two Pictures of the Pharisees: Philosophical Circle or Eating Club," *Anglican Theological Review* 64 (1982) 525–38.

3 For a different analysis of the parable of the lost sheep, see Arthur E. Zannoni, *Tell Me Your Name: Images of God in the Bible* (Chicago: Liturgy Training Publications, 2000), 55–89.

4 Mary Rose D'Angelo, "Women in Luke-Acts" *(Journal of Biblical Literature)*, 109, 1990, 441–61.

5 Recently, an interpretation has become quite popular that maintains the lost coin was part of a set of decorative coins in a bridal headdress or necklace. This interpretation makes the coin valuable because it is part of the woman's dowry or because the whole necklace loses its value if it is missing one coin. This interpretation, however, comes from the practice of modern nomadic Bedouin women, not Jewish women of the first century. See Carol Scherstsen La Hurd "Rediscovering the Lost Women in Luke 15," *(Biblical Theology Bulletin)* 24, 1994, 66–67.

6 The books and commentaries that deal with the parable of the prodigal son are innumerable. No attempt will be made here to mention all of them. However, for a deeply moving and spiritual interpretation, see Henri J. Nouwen, The *Return of the Prodigal Son: A Meditation on Fathers, Brothers and Sons*. New York: Doubleday, 1992.

Chapter Seven

1 For an analysis of the role of riches and poverty in the Bible, see Leslie J. Hoppe, *Being Poor* (Wilmington: Glazier, 1987).

2 John R. Donahue, *The Gospel in Parable* (Minneapolis: Fortress Press, 1988), 178.

3 *Ibid*, 179–180.

4 Fred B. Craddock, *Luke* (Louisville: Westminster/John Knox, 1990), 192.

5 The Lazarus mentioned in Luke's gospel is not the brother of Mary and Martha mentioned in John's gospel (11:1–57).

Chapter Eight

1 See Helen and Leonard Doohan, *Prayer in the New Testament: Make Your Requests Known to God.* (Collegeville: Liturgical Press, 1992). Robert J. Karris, *Prayer and the New Testament* (New York: Crossroad Publishing Co., 2000), 40–81.

2 For a detailed explanation of the role of honor and shame in the gospel of Luke, see J.H. Neyrey, ed., *The Social World of Luke-Acts* (Peabody: Hendrickson, 1991), 25–65.

3 Some interpreters suggest that the judge fears that the widow may give him a black eye. While such a translation of the Greek may be reading a current colloquialism back into the text, it does cause one to ponder. See Arland J. Hultgren, *The Parables of Jesus: A Commentary* (Grand Rapids: Eerdmans, 2000), 255.

4 For an excellent presentation of the contrast between the judge and the widow, see Barbara Green, *Like A Tree Planted: An Exploration of Psalms and Parables Through Metaphors* (Collegeville: Liturgical Press, 1997), 72–88.

5 Megan McKenna, *Parables: The Arrows of God* (Maryknoll, NY: Orbis, 1994), 107.

6 Green, *Like a Tree Planted*, 69.

Chapter Nine

1 For a detailed explanation of the monetary system at the time, see Kenneth Harl, *Coinage in the Roman Economy, 300 B.C. to A.D. 700* (Baltimore: John Hopkins University Press, 1996).

2 The figures being used here can only be approximate. The textual notes for the *Revised Standard Version* and the *New Revised Standard Version* say that a talent was "more than fifteen years' wages of a laborer." The note in the *New Jerusalem Bible* states that 10,000 talents were over 60 million dollars. The note in the *New International Version* records, "That is, several million dollars."

3 The traditional use of the literary genre known as the symposium can be found in the six books of *Table Talk* by Plutarch.

4 Josephus, *Jewish Wars* 4.8.3 and 2.8.4.

5 Samuel Sandmel, *Anti-Semitism in the New Testament?* (Philadelphia: Fortress Press, 1978), 104.

6 For a more detailed explanation of the tension between Jewish peasants and the Jerusalem priesthood/aristocracy, see Kenneth E. Bailey, *Through Peasant Eyes: More Lucan Parables, Their Culture and Style* (Grand Rapids: Eerdmans, 1980), 446ff.

7 Josephus, *Antiquities* 18:30.

8 Richard J. O'Dea, "A Modern Good Samaritan" *America* (vol. 180, No. 7, March 6, 1999), 18.

Chapter Ten

1 Dietrich Bonhoeffer, *The Cost of Discipleship* (New York: Macmillan Publishing Co., 1963), 63.

2 For descriptions and detailed explanations of the gospel call stories, see Dennis M. Sweetland, *Our Journey With Jesus: Discipleship According to Mark* (Wilmington, DE: Michael Glazier, 1987), and by the same author, *Our Journey With Jesus: Discipleship According to Luke-Acts* (Collegeville, MN: Liturgical Press, 1990).

3 For a detailed analysis of the role of women in the gospel of Luke, see Barbara E. Reid, *Choosing the Better Part? Women In the Gospel of Luke* (Collegeville, MN: Liturgical Press, 1996).

4 *Abot R.Nat.* 24:1; quoted from *The Fathers According to Rabbi Nathan: An Analytic Translation and Explanation*, translated by Jacob Neusner, *Brown Judaic Studies* 114 (Atlanta: Scholars Press, 1986), 149. The parable is also found in Brad Young, *Jesus and His Jewish Parables: Jewish Tradition and Christian Interpretation* (Peabody, MA: Hendrickson, 1988) 257.

5 The text of the hymn was composed by Samuel J. Stone (1839–1900) and the tune by Samuel Wesley (1810–1876). It is #661 in *Gather Comprehensive* (Chicago: GIA Publications, 1994).

6 There have been a variety of interpretations about the tower in this parable. Included among these is the interpretation that the parable calls to mind the palace Herod built in Jerusalem with three towers named for a friend, a brother and his wife. For further reading, see D.N. Freedman, "Towers" in *The Anchor Bible Dictionary*, vol. 6 (New York: Doubleday, 1992), 622–24.

7 For an excellent treatment of the meaning of grace, see Bill Huebsch, *A New Look at Grace* (Mystic, CT: Twenty Third Publications, 1996).

8 For another interpretation of the parable, which stresses more of the graciousness of God over the call to discipleship, see Arthur E. Zannoni, *Tell Me Your Name: Images of God in the Bible* (Chicago: Liturgy Training Publications, 2000), 56–57.

Bibliography

Alter, Robert and Frank Kermode, eds. *The Literary Guide to the Bible*. Cambridge, MA: Harvard University Press, 1987.

Bailey, Kenneth E. *Poet and Peasant: A Literary Cultural Approach to the Parables In Luke*. Grand Rapids, MI: Wm. B. Eerdmans, 1976, revised 1980.

———. *Through Peasant Eyes: More Lucan Parables, Their Culture and Style*. Grand Rapids, MI: Eerdmans, 1980.

Blomberg, C. *Interpreting the Parables*. Downers Grove, IL: Inter Varsity Press, 1990.

Bonhoeffer, Dietrich. *The Cost of Discipleship*. London: SCM Press, 1959.

Boucher, Madeline T. *The Parables*. Wilmington, DE: Michael Glazier, 1981.

Brown, Raymond E. *Introduction to the New Testament*. New York: Doubleday, 1997.

Capon, Robert Farrar. *The Parables of Grace*. Grand Rapids, MI: Eerdmans, 1988.

Carter, Warren and John Paul Heil. *Matthew's Parables: Audience-Oriented Perspectives*. (*Catholic Biblical Quarterly*, Series 30) Washington, DC: The Catholic Biblical Association of America, 1998.

Carlston, C.E. *The Parables of the Triple Tradition*. Philadelphia: Fortress, 1974.

Chilton, Bruce. *The Kingdom of God*. Philadelphia: Fortress, 1981.

Craddock, Fred B. *Luke*. Louisville, KY: John Knox, 1990.

Crossan, John Dominic. *Cliffs of Fall: Paradox and Polyvalence in the Parables of Jesus*. New York: Seabury, 1980.

———. *In Parables: The Challenge of the Historical Jesus*. San Francisco: Harper & Row, 1973.

Culbertson, Philip L. *A Word Fitly Spoken*. Albany: SUNY Press, 1995.

Davies, W. D. and Dale C. Alison. *A Critical and Exegetical Commentary on the Gospel According to St. Matthew*. Edinburgh: T & T Clark, 1991.

Dodd, Charles H. *The Parables of the Kingdom*. New York: Charles Scribner Sons, 1961.

Donahue, John R. *The Gospel in Parable: Metaphor, Narrative and Theology in the Synoptic Gospels*. Philadelphia: Fortress Press, 1988.

Doohan, Leonard and Helen. *Prayer in the New Testament: Make Your Requests Known to God*. Collegeville, MN: Liturgical Press, 1992.

Drury, John. *The Parables in the Gospels: History and Allegory.* New York: Crossroad, 1985.

Fisher, Neal F. *Parables of Jesus: Glimpses of God's Reign.* New York: Crossroad, 1990.

Fitzmyer, Joseph A. *The Gospel According to Luke.* (Anchor Bible, vol. 28), Garden City, NY: Doubleday, 1981.

Funk, Robert W. *Language, Hermeneutic, and the Word of God.* New York: Harper & Row, 1966.

———. Bernard Brandon Scott and James R. Butts. *The Parables of Jesus: Red Letter Edition. A Report of the Jesus Seminar.* Sonoma, CA: Polebridge, 1988.

———. *Parables and Presence.* Philadelphia: Fortress, 1982.

Gowler, David B. *What Are They Saying About the Parables?* Mahwah, NJ: Paulist Press, 2000.

Green, Barbara. *Like A Tree Planted: An Exploration of Psalms and Parables Through Metaphor.* Collegeville, MN: Liturgical Press, 1997.

Hanson, Kenneth. *Dead Sea Scrolls: The Untold Story.* Tulsa, OK: Council Oak Books, 1997.

Hedrick, Charles. *Parables as Poetic Fictions: The Creative Voice of Jesus.* Peabody, MA: Hendrickson, 1994.

Hellwig, Monika. *Jesus the Compassion of God.* Wilmington, DE: Michael Glazier, 1983.

Hendrickx, H. *The Parables of Jesus.* San Francisco: Harper & Row, 1986.

Hennecke, E. and Schneermelcher, W. *New Testament Apocrypha,* vol. 1. London: 1963-65.

Herzog, W. *Parables as Subversive Speech.* Louisville: Westminster/John Knox, 1994.

Hones, Ivor H. *The Matthean Parables: A Literary and Historical Commentary.* Leiden: Brill, 1995.

Hoppe, Leslie J. *Being Poor.* Wilmington, DE: Michael Glazier, 1987.

Hoover, James. *Mark: Follow Me.* Downers Grove, IL: Inter Varsity, 1985.

Huebsch, Bill. *A New Look at Grace.* Mystic, CT: Twenty Third Publications, 1996.

Hughes, John Jay. *Stories Told: Modern Meditations on the Parables.* Liguori, MO: Liguori Press, 1998.

Hultgren, Arland J. *The Parables of Jesus: A Commentary.* Grand Rapids, MI: Wm. B. Eerdmans, 2000.

Hunter, A.M. *Interpreting the Parables.* London: SCM, 1960.

Imbach, Joseph. *And He Taught Them With Pictures: The Parables in Practice Today.* Springfield, IL: Templeton Publishers, 1997.

Jeremias, Joachim. *Rediscovering the Parables.* New York: Charles Scribner's Sons, 1966.

———. *The Parables of Jesus.* London: SCM, 1962.

Johnson, Elizabeth. *She Who Is.* New York: Crossroad, 1992.

Jones, Geriant Vaughn. *The Art and Truth of the Parables.* London: SPCK, 1964.

Jones, Ivor H. *The Matthean Parables: A Literary and Historical Commentary.* Leiden: Brill, 1995.

Karl, Kenneth. *Coinage in the Roman Economy, 300 BC to AD 700.* Baltimore: John Hopkins University Press, 1996.

Karris, Robert J. *Prayer and the New Testament.* New York: Crossroad Publishing Co., 2000.

Keating, T. *The Kingdom of God in Luke.* New York: Crossroad, 1993.

Kingsbury, Jack D. *The Parables of Jesus in Matthew 13.* St. Louis: Clayton, 1969.

Kissinger, Warren S. *The Parables of Jesus: A History of Interpretation and Bibliography.* Metuchen, NJ, and London: Scarecrow, 1979.

Kjargaard, Morgens Stiller. *Metaphor and Parable.* Leiden: Brill, 1986.

Lambrecht, Jan. *Out of the Treasure: The Parables in the Gospel of Matthew.* Louvain: Peters; Grand Rapids: Eerdmans, 1992.

———. *Once More Astonished: The Parables of Jesus.* New York: Crossroad, 1981.

LaVediere, Eugene. *Dining in the Kingdom of God.* Chicago: Liturgy Training Publications, 1994.

Linnemann, Eta. *The Jesus of the Parables: Introduction and Exposition.* London: SPCK, 1966.

Manson, T.W. *The Teachings of Jesus: Studies of Its Form and Content.* Cambridge: Cambridge University Press, 1948.

Martini, Carlo. *The Spiritual Journey of the Apostles.* Boston: St. Paul Books and Media, 1991.

Mazziotta, Richard. *Jesus in the Gospels, Old Stories Told Anew.* Notre Dame, IN: Ave Maria Press, 1986.

Mays, James L. *Harper's Bible Commentary.* San Francisco: Harper & Row, 1988.

McArthur, Harvey K. and Johnson, Robert M. *They Also Taught In Parables from the First Century to the Christian Era.* Grand Rapids: Zondervan, 1990.

McFague, S. *Speaking in Parables: A Study in Metaphor and Theology.* Philadelphia: Fortress, 1975.

McKenna, Megan. *Parables: The Arrows of God*. Maryknoll, NY: Orbis Books, 1994.

Miller, John W. *Step by Step Through the Bible*. New York: Paulist, 1981.

Neusner, Jacob. *Brown Judaic Studies*. Atlanta: Scholars Press, 1986.

Neyrey, J.H., ed. *The Social World of Luke Acts*. Peabody: Hendrickson, 1991.

Nouwen, Henri J. *The Return of the Prodigal Son: A Meditation on Fathers, Brothers, and Sons*. New York: Doubleday, 1992.

"Parable" in the *Anchor Bible Dictionary*. New York: Doubleday, 1992.

"Parable" in the *Collegeville Pastoral Dictionary of Biblical Theology*. Collegeville: Liturgical Press, 1996.

"Parable" in *Harper's Bible Dictionary*. San Francisco: Harper & Row, 1985.

Parker, Andrew. *Painfully Clear: The Parables of Jesus*. Sheffield: Sheffield Academic Press, 1996.

Perkins, Pheme. *Hearing the Parables of Jesus*. Mahwah, NJ: Paulist Press, 1981.

Perrin, Norman. *Jesus and the Language of the Kingdom*. Philadelphia: Fortress Press, 1976.

Reid, Barbara E. *Choosing the Better Part? Women In the Gospel of Luke*. Collegeville, MN: Liturgical Press, 1996.

———. *Parables for Preachers: Year B*. Collegeville, MN: Liturgical Press, 1999.

———. *Parables for Preachers: Year C*. Collegeville, MN: Liturgical Press, 2000.

Sandmel, Samuel. *Anti-Semitism in the New Testament?* Philadelphia: Fortress Press, 1978.

Scott, Bernard Brandon. *Hear Then the Parables: A Commentary on the Parables of Jesus*. Minneapolis: Fortress Press, 1989.

———. *Jesus, Symbol-Maker for the Kingdom*. Philadelphia: Fortress Press, 1981.

Shea, John. *Stories of Faith*. Chicago: Thomas More Press, 1978.

———. *Gospel Light*. New York: Crossroad Publishing Co., 1998.

Shermis, Michael and Arthur E. Zannoni, eds. *Introduction to Jewish Christian Relations*. Mahwah, NJ.: Paulist Press, 1991.

Sider, John W. *Interpreting the Parables: A Hermeneutical Guide to Their Meaning*. Grand Rapids, MI: Zondervan, 1995.

Shillington, V. George, ed. *Jesus and His Parables*. Edinburgh: T&T Clark, 1997.

Snodgrass, Klyne R. *The Parable of the Wicked Tenants: An Inquiry Into Parable Interpretation*. Tubingen: Mohr-Siebeck, 1983.

Stein, Robert H. *The Method and Message of Jesus' Teachings*. Louisville: Westminster, 1994.

————. *An Introduction to the Parables of Jesus*. Philadelphia: Westminster Press, 1981.

Stern, David. *Parables and Midrash*. Cambridge, MA: Harvard University Press, 1991.

Thoma, Clemens and Michael Wyschogrod, eds. *Parable and Story in Judaism and Christianity*. New York: Paulist Press, 1989.

Thurston, Bonnie. *Women in the New Testament*. New York: Crossroad, 1998.

Tolbert, M.A. *Perspectives on the Parables*. Philadelphia: Fortress, 1979.

Via, D.O. *The Parables: Their Literary and Existential Dimension*. Philadelphia: Fortress, 1967.

Wenham, David. *The Parables of Jesus*. Downers Grove: Intervarsity, 1989.

Westerman, Claus. *The Parables of Jesus in Light of the Old Testament*. Minneapolis: Fortress Press, 1990.

Wiesel, Elie. *The Gates of the Forest*. New York: Holt, Rinehart and Winston, 1966.

Wilder, Amos. *The Language of the Gospel*. New York: Harper & Row, 1971.

Young, Brad H. *Jesus and His Jewish Parables: Rediscovering the Roots of Jesus' Teaching*. New York: Paulist Press, 1989.

————. *The Parables: Jewish Tradition and Christian Interpretation*. Peabody, Mass: Hendrickson Publishers, 1999.

Zannoni, Arthur E. *Tell Me Your Name: Images of God in the Bible*. Chicago: Liturgy Training Publications, 2000.

————. *Jesus of the Gospels: Teacher, Storyteller, Friend, Messiah*. Cincinnati, Ohio: St. Anthony Messenger Press, 1996.

————, ed. *Jews and Christians Speak of Jesus*. Minneapolis: Fortress, 1994.

Index of Scripture References